RE-READING THE SHORT STORY

Also by Clare Hanson

KATHERINE MANSFIELD (*with Andrew Gurr*)
SHORT STORIES AND SHORT FICTIONS, 1880–1980
THE CRITICAL WRITINGS OF KATHERINE MANSFIELD (*editor*)

Re-reading the Short Story

Edited by

CLARE HANSON
Senior Lecturer in English
College of St Paul and St Mary, Cheltenham

St. Martin's Press New York

First published in the United States of America in 1989

Printed in China

ISBN 0–312–02398–7

Library of Congress Cataloging-in-Publication Data
Re-reading the short story.
Includes bibliographies.
1. Short story—Congresses. 2. Short stories, English—History and criticism—Congresses.
3. Short stories, American—History and criticism—Congresses. I. Hanson, Clare.
PN3373.R5 1989 809.3′1 88–18402
ISBN 0–312–02398–7

Contents

Notes on the Contributors

Nicola Bradbury is Lecturer in English at the University of Reading. Her publications include *Henry James: The Later Novels* (1979) and *A Select Bibliography of Henry James* (1986).

Mary Eagleton lectures in Literature at the College of Ripon and York St John. She has been closely involved in the development of Women's Studies and is the editor of *Feminist Literary Theory: A Reader* (1986).

Robert Hampson is Lecturer in English at Royal Holloway and Bedford New College, University of London.

Clare Hanson is Lecturer in English at the College of St Paul and St Mary, Cheltenham. Her publications include *Short Stories and Short Fictions, 1880–1980* (1985) and, as editor, *The Critical Writings of Katherine Mansfield* (1987).

Nicole Ward Jouve is Reader in English at the University of York. She is the author of two novels, *Le Spectre du Gris* (translated by herself as *Shades of Grey*, 1981) and *L'Entremise* (1980). She is the author too of a critical work on Baudelaire, *A Fire to Conquer Darkness* (1980). She has written numerous articles, especially on women's writing, and has recently published a study of the Yorkshire Ripper (*The Streetcleaner: The Yorkshire Ripper on Trial*, 1986). She has also published a book on Colette (1987).

Lionel Kelly teaches English at the University of Reading. His special interests are 18th-century and modern English literature, and 20th-century American literature. He is the editor of *Tobias Smollett* in the Routledge Critical Heritage series, and of *Richard Aldington, Papers from the Reading Conference*.

David Miall is Senior Lecturer in English at the College of St Paul and St Mary, Cheltenham. He is the author of many articles on literary theory and hermeneutics, contributing to the *British Journal of Psychology* as well as to specialist literary journals.

Jean Pickering is Professor of English at California State University, Fresno. Apart from publishing her own short stories, she has contributed to G. K. Hall & Co's forthcoming seven-volume history of the short story, and has written on English women writers, including Vera Brittain and Margaret Drabble.

Ellen Cronan Rose is Associate Professor of English at Drexel University, Philadelphia. Her publications include *Margaret Drabble: Equivocal Figures* (1980) and several essays on Doris Lessing. She is currently preparing a handbook on *The Golden Notebook* for the Modern Language Association.

Claire Sprague is Visiting Professor of English at New York University. She is the editor of *Twentieth Century Views: Virginia Woolf* (1971) and, with Virginia Tiger, of *Critical Essays on Doris Lessing* (1986). She has recently published a critical study, *Rereading Doris Lessing* (1987) and is the editor of the *Doris Lessing Newsletter*.

1

Introduction

CLARE HANSON

For a complex of reasons the short story has been largely excluded from the arena of contemporary critical debate: this collection of essays aims to re-establish the short story as a legitimate subject for discussion. Each of the essays was first presented at a Symposium on the Short Story held at the College of St Paul and St Mary, Cheltenham, in September 1986. The idea for the symposium came from a general feeling of dissatisfaction with the current level of debate on the short story form. Some of the contributors had previously worked on the short story, and all shared a sense that a unique area of literary activity was being neglected in critical terms – and this, paradoxically, at a time when it seemed that the short story would prove a particularly fruitful area of study in the light of recent developments in literary theory. In this introduction I have attempted to chart some of the reasons for this paradoxical situation. It caused mixed feelings of exhilaration and frustration for the contributors to this collection: exhilaration at working on such an untouched area; frustration at seeing a wide communication gap and feeling a need to persuade others of the importance of a field which was becoming almost ghettoised. The publication of these essays is a step towards bridging this gap, making for necessary communication.

Why has the short story been neglected, in both academic and non-academic critical circles? It is a form, after all, which is immensely popular with readers, and, perhaps more importantly, with writers. Doris Lessing, for example, confesses, as Ellen Rose points out in her essay in this collection, to an 'addiction' to the short story form. Does the problem lie in the fact that the short story is not quite respectable as an art form precisely *because* it is 'popular' in the pejorative sense? It took a long while for the novel to establish itself as a 'serious' art form: the short story – a relatively recent form – is still struggling. Also, the phenomenal success of the 'woman's short story' in the weekly magazines – comparable to the success of Mills and Boon fiction – has undoubtedly helped to fix the form as popular and/or inferior in the minds of literary critics. Because of the economic difficulties of short story publishing, even the more serious new writers, Tama Janowitz for example, appear not only in the prestigious *New Yorker* but in the more humdrum British *Woman's Journal*: so in the late 20th century the short story form is still tied to the magazine outlet and to a potentially disabling publishing context.

Over the last ten years a handful of academic books have grappled with the thorny question of short story theory.[1] However, the best theory and criticism of the short story form has come from practising writers: Frank O'Connor, for example, in his pioneering study *The Lonely Voice* (1963); Eudora Welty in her subtle and oblique *The Eye of the Story* (1978). Nadine Gordimer, too, contributing to the 1968 *Kenyon Review* 'International Symposium on the Short Story' has pointed suggestively to the special possibilities of the short story form:

> Each of us has a thousand lives and a novel gives a character only one. *For the sake of the form*. The novelist may juggle about with chronology and throw narrative overboard; all the time his characters have the reader by the hand, there is a consistency of relationship throughout the experience that cannot and does not convey the quality of human life, where contact is more like the flash of fire-flies, in and out, now here, now there, in darkness. Short story writers see by the light of the flash; theirs is the art of the only thing one can be sure of – the present moment. Ideally, they have learned to do without explanation of what went before, and what happens beyond this point.[2]

A further point suggests itself. Is it not the case that the short story is or has been notably a form of the margins, a form which is in some sense ex-centric, not part of official or 'high' cultural hegemony? If by literary form itself we mean the expectations which we as readers bring to a genre, then the form of the short story has lent itself to the presentation of the partial, the incomplete, that which cannot be, as Nadine Gordimer suggests, entirely satisfactorily organised or 'explained'. The short story has offered itself to losers and loners, exiles, women, blacks – writers who for one reason or another have not been part of the ruling 'narrative' or epistemological/experiential framework of their society. So

Frank O'Connor explains the way in which the short story may speak for the individual who has become detached from his society: in *The Lonely Voice* he argues that,

> Always in the short story there is this sense of outlawed figures wandering about the fringes of society, superimposed sometimes on symbolic figures whom they caricature and echo – Christ, Socrates, Moses . . . Clearly, the novel and the short story, though they derive from the same sources, derive in a quite different way, and are distinct literary forms; and the difference is not so much formal (though, as we shall see, there are plenty of formal differences) as ideological. I am not, of course, suggesting that for the future the short story can be written only by Eskimos and American Indians: without going so far afield, we have plenty of submerged population groups. I am suggesting strongly that we can see in it an attitude of mind that is attracted by submerged population groups, whatever these may be at any given time – tramps, artists, lonely idealists, dreamers and spoiled priests. The novel can still adhere to the classical concept of civilised society, of man as an animal who lives in a community, as in Jane Austen and Trollope it obviously does; *but the short story remains by its very nature remote from society – romantic, individualistic, and intransigent.*[3] [Emphasis added]

The short story has been too the chosen form of the exile – not the self-willed *émigré,* but the writer who longs to return to a home culture which is denied him / her. Katherine Mansfield is probably the most famous example: she might easily be paired with Jean Rhys, who wrote with similarly ambiguous feelings about her irrecoverable Caribbean home. Nadine Gordimer and Doris Lessing offer more recent examples of writers exiled in this double sense: exiled literally or physically from their home country, and exiled internally in their adopted country and culture.[4] For such writers, the short story has offered a prime means of expression.

The last four writers mentioned are of course women, and I would suggest that the short story has been from its inception a particularly appropriate vehicle for the expression of the ex-centric, alienated vision of women. It is striking, for example, to see the way in which the early 'modern' short story, in the form of the psychological sketch, was taken over by women writers during the era of the New Woman of the 1880s and 1890s. Writers such as

George Egerton, Ella D'Arcy and Evelyn Sharp saw the potential offered by the form for the exploration of uncharted or hidden areas of women's subjective experience. I think that the idea of something 'hidden' is important, too, as is suggested by the title of Hermione Lee's fine anthology of stories by women, *The Secret Self* (1985). (The title comes from a letter of Katherine Mansfield to the painter Dorothy Brett, from 1921: 'One tries to go deep – to speak to the secret self we all have – to acknowledge that'). In her introduction to *The Secret Self* Hermione Lee concludes somewhat regretfully that 'it doesn't seem profitable, then, to pursue a separatist aesthetic theory of the twentieth-century woman's short story': it may lead women back, she argues, into a separatist ghetto. Yet surely it is important to register and define the 'difference of view' which has existed historically for women writers in the 19th and 20th centuries, and which has been expressed particularly through their short stories? An investigation of difference and of the 'muffled consciousness' of women is by no means the same thing as an assertion that difference, or oppression, is in any sense essential or desirable.

It is perhaps significant too that since the publication of *The Secret Self* another major anthology of stories solely by women writers has been published, *Wayward Girls and Wicked Women*, edited by Angela Carter. Carter stresses the similarities between the stories she has chosen, diverse as they are in subject matter and period:

> All the stories I have chosen are reflections in some kind of squinting, oblique, penetrating vision. (Some of them are also very funny.)[5]

In their Introduction to another collection of short stories by women,[6] *Everyday Matters* (London: Sheba, 1982) the editors comment:

> The stories we chose were those that made us laugh or shudder, reminded us of something or made us think again about our own lives and the lives of other women. But these stories have one thing in common: they do not sit comfortably. In one way or another each of them questions or resists the story we were all told from earliest days – the story which told us how we feel and what we want and who we are.[7]

In other words the short story is the preferred form for those women writers who have what in conventional terms would be viewed as a 'squint vision'. Such writers see things differently from men – hence the potential charge of distortion. They also express what would otherwise remain hidden: a sense of alienation from dominant culture and ideology which may be frightening in its intensity. The short story can present such alienation more effectively than a novel: the choice of the novel form must involve the writer (no matter how revolutionary his/her intentions) in certain epistemological and ideological assumptions which would not readily be tolerated by the wayward girls and wicked women lovingly selected by Angela Carter.

Without labouring the point, it is clear that the short story form has offered particular opportunities for suppressed or, in O'Connor's word, 'submerged' groups in society – black writers in America, for example, or homosexual writers. The short story has been a particularly important form for black *women* writers in America – Zora Neale Hurston (her early stories have just been republished by the Camden Press); Paule Marshall (*Merle and Other Stories*); Alice Walker (*In Love and Trouble* and *You Can't Keep a Good Woman Down*); most recently Gloria Naylor in *The Women of Brewster Place*. These women of course suffer from a double oppression, sexual and racial.

If, as I suggest, the short story is a marginal form, this will, to return to an earlier point, partly explain why there has been relatively little critical writing about it, relatively little speculation. It is also true that, as Nicola Bradbury points out in her essay in this collection, it can be a mistake to search for *a* theory of the short story form, as though one theory could compass the diversity of writing practices covered by the term 'short story'. It can be argued that the short story has no inherent, determining characteristics, though we may discern tendencies, especially if we place the form in its historical context. For, as Walter Allen has suggested,[8] the short story as we know it is a modern form. Elizabeth Bowen has called it the 'child of this century': it first flowered in the 1890s, and then developed, as Bowen has pointed out, hand-in-glove with the cinema. The link between the two forms may be more than fortuitous: in an essay of 1937 Elizabeth Bowen listed techniques which the two forms had in common ('oblique narration, cutting, the unlikely placing of emphasis'), and then went on to suggest deeper affinities:

> The new literature, whether written or visual, is an affair of reflexes, of immediate susceptibility, of associations not examined by reason: it does not attempt a synthesis. Narrative of any length involves continuity, sometimes a forced continuity: it is here that the novel too often becomes invalid.[9]

It is interesting to consider the reciprocal relation between the short story and film, both forms which have altered our conception of narrative. Both short story and film reject or deny certain levels of narrative, a certain kind of discursive 'explanation', preferring instead to work on a level on which unconscious desires and motives may be explored via 'associations not examined by reason'. It may be that both short story and film are modelled in part on the structure of the unconscious, which exists, Lacan suggests, in an asymmetrical relation to the dominant structure of language. In my own essay in this collection I take as a starting point the idea that the short story may partake of the worlds of both what Lacan would call the 'imaginary' and the 'symbolic', the unconscious and language, and try to suggest some of the difficulties involved in such trafficking between image and narrative.

It is an assumption shared, then, by the contributors to this volume that the short story is a highly distinctive art form, different in kind, not in degree, from its sister form the novel. The short story is a vehicle for different *kinds* of knowledge, knowledge which may be in some way at odds with the 'story' of dominant culture. The formal properties of the short story – disjunction, inconclusiveness, obliquity – connect with its ideological marginality and with the fact that the form may be used to express something suppressed/repressed in mainstream literature. We might put it one way by saying that the short story gives us the other side of 'the official story' or narrative, or we might suggest that the short story suggests that which cannot normally be said, hence its close connection, in form and content, with fantasy, which is another mode of expression for repressed desire or knowledge.

These are wide generalisations: not all stories, clearly, work like this. Yet it is worth considering the way in which many novelists have used the short story form to express something which, they felt, could not be expressed in a novel. It is instructive to find Elizabeth Bowen, for example – an artist whom many consider a finer short story writer than a novelist – writing of the way in which the supernatural (defined as 'happenings unable to be rationally explained') can find its way into her stories but not, for some reason, into her novels (it should be stressed that the supernatural is particularly important to her, too):

> I would point out that a number of my stories, such as *The Demon Lover, The Cheery Soul, Hand in Glove, The Happy Autumn Fields*, have a supernatural element in them, which makes some of the happenings unable to be rationally explained. I do not make use of the supernatural as a get-out; it is inseparable (whether or not it comes to the surface) from my sense of life. That I feel it unethical – for some reason? – to allow the supernatural into a novel may be one of my handicaps as a sincere novelist.[10]

A further issue, raised by Nicole Ward Jouve in her essay in this collection, is that of the relation between the short story and the book. It is an important question in two senses. Of course, we know that many short story collections work *designedly* in some sense as a whole, the different stories interpenetrating and, often retrospectively, illuminating each other. Examples would be Sherwood Anderson's *Winesburg, Ohio*; Joyce's *Dubliners*, V. S. Naipaul's *Miguel Street*, Alice Munro's *The Beggar Maid*. The link is very often forged out of unity of place or of narrative perspective. On the other hand, stories are often specifically intended *not* to be read in sequence or order, and the order in which they end up in a collection may often be very largely the publisher's creation. To what extent is this a 'betrayal' of the original energy and impetus of the free-standing short story form? It may be that one of the important things which the short story does is to challenge the 'tyranny of the whole book' in this sense, to challenge the idea of the book as necessarily unified, complete, in some small sense representing, standing (in) metonymically for a complete, unified world.

This collection of essays refuses, too, unity, consensus. The essays here differ widely in theoretical assumptions and bias: editorial design extends only so far to suggest a reading of the essays as in two distinct groups, the first group being theoretical in orientation, the second more text-based. The essays do in fact fall conveniently into two groups of five. The first essay, by David Miall, offers a model of story understanding, exploring the ways in which affective modes supervene over information-based modes of comprehension. Clare Hanson offers notes towards a poetics of short fiction, suggesting in particular that there are important analogies between the structure of dreams and the structure of short stories. Nicole Ward Jouve tackles the difficult question of what might aptly be called the existential problem of length in prose fiction, starting from the position of one who is a practising writer as well as critic: this leads into Jean Pickering's exploration, from a similar perspective, of the relations between the short story and the novel form. Mary Eagleton's essay concludes this section by taking up the question of the relations between gender and genre in the short story context.

Robert Hampson's essay on the short stories of Sylvia Plath and Alice Munro opens the next section: he explores the 'pleasures of disruption' in specific texts. Nicola Bradbury offers a reading of the stories of John McGahern which unites attentiveness to particular texts and theoretical vigour. Lionel Kelly offers a persuasive reading of stories by Fitzgerald and Hemingway. The last two essays offer distinct but complementary views of the large body of short stories produced by Doris Lessing.

It remains for us all to thank the colleagues and students who participated in the Symposium on the Short Story, providing us with a genuine forum for debate.

Notes

1. See, for example, Walter Allen, *The Short Story in English* (Oxford University Press, 1981); Clare Hanson, *Short Stories and Short Fictions, 1880–1980* (London: Macmillan, 1985); Valerie Shaw, *The Short Story: A Critical Introduction* (London: Longman, 1983). Since this book went to press, John Bayley has published *The Short Story: Henry James to Elizabeth Bowen* (Brighton: Harvester, 1988).
2. Nadine Gordimer in 'The International Symposium on the Short Story', *Kenyon Review*, vol. 30 (1968) p. 459.
3. Frank O'Connor, *The Lonely Voice: A Study of the Short Story* (London: Macmillan, 1963).
4. For an exploration of the implications of such an exile see Andrew Gurr, *Writers in Exile* (Brighton: Harvester, 1981).
5. Angela Carter (ed.), *Wayward Girls and Wicked Women* (London: Virago, 1986).
6. Further recent collections of short stories by women include *Original Prints: New Writing from Scottish Women* (Edinburgh: Polygon Books,

1985); *Passion Fruit: Romantic Fiction with a Twist* (London: Pandora, 1986).
7. *Everyday Matters*, 'Introduction', p. ix.
8. Walter Allen, *The Short Story in English*, op. cit., p. 3.
9. *The Faber Book of Modern Stories*, ed. with an Introduction by Elizabeth Bowen (London: Faber & Faber, 1937), p. 7.
10. Elizabeth Bowen, 'Preface' to *A Day in the Dark and Other Stories* (London: Jonathan Cape, 1965) p. 9.

2

Text and Affect: A Model of Story Understanding

DAVID MIALL

THE DEFAMILIARISATION MODEL OF NARRATIVE

One standard approach to narrative which is, I take it, derived from Romantic theory, runs through the Russian Formalists, and into current views such as those of Perry and Iser.[1] For shorthand I shall call it the defamiliarisation model. It assumes that there is a set of norms and conventions which the text calls into play, only to unsettle them in some way and point to an alternative interpretation of reality, or (in some modernist texts) the impossibility of interpretation in itself. I have adopted this model of narrative as the framework for my own exploration, although I shall have some critical things to say about some of its assumptions, which seem to me to be in need of revision.

This approach also states that a text is not a self-sufficient, autonomous entity: it requires realisation, a conscious input from the reader. A story is what Ingarden[2] called a heteronomous object: its meaning is immanent until it is made concrete in the act of reading. If you look at studies of reader response, however, one aspect of reading is usually missing: the emotional one. While theorists make gestures towards the interest and involvement of the reader, this is generally allowed no place as a theoretical construct in how responses to texts are formulated. It could be said, then, that the models of the reader offered by literary theorists, such as Riffaterre's 'superreader', Iser's 'implied reader', Brooke-Rose's 'encoded reader',[3] and the like, are too cognitive, and lay down too much of an ideal: they specify a textual process which exerts a determining power on any reader. It is also worth noting that the considerable individual differences between readers that occur in practice remain unaccounted for in such models. I shall offer another view, which builds on the notion of the implied reader; but I would prefer to speak more simply of the 'interested reader'.

There is of course an alternative approach to reader response, which centres on subjective aspects of reading: this is to be found in the work of Norman Holland and David Bleich.[4] Holland's pursuit of reader involvement turns on his concept that each reader brings his 'identity theme' to the reading. But this, in brief, can be criticised for being an essentially static conception, in which no important changes in the reader are initiated by the text. Holland's construct also implies a stable, unified ego: as Culler points out, Holland 'has transferred the concept of unity from text to person'.[5] A third difficulty is that in Holland's account texts can have no intrinsic structure of meaning. For Holland the meaning of a text lies in the responses made to it, and his study of response statements leads him to say that statements about the same text 'have practically nothing in common'. Any sameness in readings comes merely from the sameness in the resources used to create the reading experience, that is, from the reader rather than the text.[6] My own work, in contrast, has suggested an intrinsic structure which is, however, differentially coloured by each reader (see below). Thus, in Holland there is an emphasis on emotion and on the self, but the structural features of the text have largely disappeared.

Holland does remind us that emotion is likely to be important in response to texts, and that there will be individual differences in response. But we have yet to explain the role of emotions. Is emotion merely an after-effect, an epiphenomenon of reading? I don't think so. I suggest that emotion plays a crucial role in the formative aspects of the reading process itself. This view should enable us to offer an alternative account of some current issues in the study of narratives. I shan't be concerned at this stage to offer ways of distinguishing different types of narrative structure or different aims with the short story, as Clare Hanson[7] does, although I think this would be a possible and fruitful extension of the approach I take. What I want to offer is a view in which emotion plays a central role in the structuring of response.

THREE ASPECTS OF EMOTION

I shall be pointing to three aspects of emotion which suggest ways of understanding response to narratives. Emotion is self-referential, it enables cross-domain linking, and above all it acts in an anticipatory manner – it is the vehicle for predictions. I will be explaining how these three features cast a useful light on some of the phenomena of interest in a theory of narrative. In addition, since practically all narratives involve characters, we can expect to find that a reader's interpretive strategies will demonstrate features in common with what we know about interpreting real people and social episodes.[8] If emotion plays a central role in social understanding, as recent research has shown, then it makes sense to suppose that emotion is central to reader response too. This approach is also free of certain awkward presuppositions inherited from the New Critical belief in the autonomy and / or unity of the text and / or the self. These can become an explicit part of the theory, subject to an appropriate critique. I have no doubt that the unity of the self is a working (if well hidden) assumption of most readers. By understanding that its basis lies in the nature of the emotions we can better account for its role in reading.

What are readers doing in emotional terms when they read? Here I return to the defamiliarisation model, to indicate how emotion enters in a formative role. Following Perry we can describe the process of reading as involving two major aspects: (1) relating the text to knowledge of the world, to codes, frames, schemata and so on; and (2) the sequential, experiential aspect of reading, the series of rhetorical effects that require the reader's interpretive activity, in which frames may be shifted, transformed or superseded. The model of Iser points to the same process: the given schemata of the 'primary code' are transcended through the reader's activity in creating the secondary, or 'aesthetic' code, such activity being a search for a more adequate knowledge to relate the given parts of the text. Roland Barthes likewise talks of the proairetic and cultural codes and the hermeneutic code respectively.[9] Thus, as Iser puts it, 'As we read, we oscillate to a greater or lesser degree between the building and breaking of illusions' – there is a defamiliarising of the reader's knowledge. What is the 'new experience' gained by the overthrowing of our standard frames of reference? In the modernist text, as well as (perhaps) many earlier ones, there is an overthrowing of our 'frames', or at least a bracketing or suspension of them. It is our experience of this process which, according to Iser, impels a reshaping of the self.[10]

It is the inadequacy of the frames, or conflicts between them, that impel the reader's hermeneutic effort. No frame can be exhaustive: the reader must fill the gaps, infer information which is not specified in the text. More significantly, a frame serves as a reference point against which to check incoming information, in which case, as Perry remarks, 'deviation from it becomes perceptible and requires motivation by another frame or principle'.[11] It is through the gap produced by an inadequacy or conflict in frames that emotion enters as a guiding force. Since the reader's frames or norms have been implicated, his interests are at stake: his motives for holding them are now in question. As other studies have shown,[12] when no coherent schema is available and the reader is in a state of uncertainty, it is the affective response which takes over. This is because of the three aspects of emotion I referred to above: self-reference, domain-crossing and anticipation. It is through these functions of emotion that the text is transformed and reconstituted at the 'aesthetic' level. I shall now turn to two studies of my own with readers of stories, which will give examples of these three functions of emotion.

STORY/ARTICLE DIFFERENCES IN AFFECT

In the first study I wanted to compare responses to a story and an article. I reasoned that expository prose was likely to be concerned mainly with presenting and elaborating a specific frame or set of frames, in contrast to a story, which is concerned to supersede the frames it presents. Thus it should be possible to detect structural differences in the role of the affective elements in each text, both those which are explicitly written into the text, and those that readers report as a part of their response.

For this study I chose two texts which were equated as far as possible, in order that differences due to the reading process rather than to content might be more easily identified. Both texts were by Virginia Woolf. The story was 'A Summing Up' which is the last story in *A Haunted House*, and the article was 'The Patron and the Crocus' which occurs in *The Common Reader*.[13] A major reason for choosing these texts is that in the first sections of each there is a balance of affective and neutral phrases. The story concerns Sasha Latham, who is led from Mrs Dalloway's party into the garden by Bertram Pritchard. Her perceptions of the garden as a magic place are shattered by Bertram when she is led to glance over the wall. The article is on the difficulties of identifying and writing for an audience.

What I did was to ask students to read either the story or the article. I had 32 students in all, of whom 15 read the story and 17 the article. They were given only the opening section of the text at first, and asked to make free written comments on it. Then they had to arrange the phrases of the opening section in order of importance (44 phrases in all, of which I had classified 13 as affective and 31 as neutral before the study). They went on to read the rest of the story, after which they made further comments on the text as a whole. Finally they reordered the phrases from the opening section again. I wanted to see what shifts, if any, took place in the importance assigned to the various phrases; I also wanted to compare the types of free response made to a story and an article. The view of emotion I have described led me to examine the data in several ways.

First, comparing responses to the story and the article, I hypothesised that readers of the story were likely to give more weight to affective elements in the text compared with readers of the article. If a story leads to some questioning of the reader's knowledge, the resulting affective response in the reader would lead him to concentrate attention on the affective elements of the text for clues to resolve the uncertainty. This turned out to be the case. The 13 affective phrases in the story were given significantly higher ratings for importance. (I use the word 'significant' here in the statistical sense.)

Secondly, if expectations in the story were generated by affective rather than cognitive factors, the more a reader showed an awareness of affect the more predictions he should make; in the case of the article, there should be no such relationship. Again, this turned out to be true. When the free comments for the story were analysed, there was a significant correlation between comments recording affective responses, and comments inferring how the story was expected to continue. Readers of the article, on the other hand, made very few affective comments, and they made no predictive inferences at all.[14]

Thirdly, predictions made at the outset while reading the first page of a story are subsumed into the reader's understanding of the story as a whole at the point he finishes his reading: what begins in affective terms becomes more cognitive as the 'point' of the story is realised. This will lead to a revision in the view of the opening part of the story: less weight will now be given to affective aspects and more to the cognitive. In other words there should be a measurable shift down in importance for the affective phrases, when these are ordered the second time. This was also found to be the case. For the article, by contrast, the affective phrases were rated overall at the same level as the neutral phrases, and neither showed a shift up or down.

A fourth implication of defamiliarising the reader's frames of reference is that the reader's motives for holding to such frames come into question. This was probably apparent in another feature of the free comments: most of the story readers mentioned being aware of themselves as readers, reacting for or against the story. Among the remarks showing motivation were 'one's inquisitiveness is aroused', 'an enthusiasm for the description', 'one wants to know more', or one 'feels frustrated at lack of information regarding the plot'. The story readers also showed they were more aware of themselves during the response by using the pronoun 'I' twice as frequently as the article readers.

Having found these signs of affect at work in structuring response to the story, I also made a detailed analysis of the shifts in the importance of the phrases. I was looking for evidence that frames postulated in the opening section of the story had been jettisoned at the end. The main conclusion I came to was that the relationship schema, which most readers imposed on Bertram and Sasha at the outset, had been replaced by one relating to Sasha's isolation and loneliness at the end. In line with this, a number of the phrases describing Bertram's 'immaterial' qualities decreased in ranked importance. Three readers, however, were unable to achieve this shift in understanding: they wrote in their final comments of being confused or disconcerted, which suggested that their attempts to elaborate an adequate view of the story as a whole had been frustrated.

This set of findings offers support for two of the three points I made about affect: that affect is self-referential and anticipatory. I also suggested that affect can bring about cross-domain links. If the reader is required to develop some novel view to understand the story, the elements of this view must be derived from his existing knowledge, but reconfigure that knowledge in some way. The opening frames have been jettisoned, thus an alternative understanding must be created from hints and suggestions scattered across the story. This is a metaphoric, rather than a metonymic process (especially in modernist fiction). The axis of selection, I would argue, is determined by the affective resonance of the frames that exist in suspension. As in an actual metaphor, this process is one of domain crossing. The subject (who in Woolf's fiction is Sasha) is reconfigured by the affect transferred to it from previously unrelated domains (here, the bestial and embattled separateness of the world beyond the garden). This process does not happen all at once, near the end of the story; it is latent, a possible response, almost from the beginning. Traces of this can be seen, again, in the relationship of certain ambivalent phrases in the opening section, as judged by these readers. Only one reader, however, explicitly anticipated that such a disillusioning outcome for Sasha was possible.

CLASSIFYING SOCIAL EPISODES

I will say a little more about the theoretical implications of this approach in a moment. I want first to mention briefly one other study I made, which looks at the domain crossing of affect more directly. As I said earlier, social psychologists have traditionally analyzed people's understanding of other people in strictly cognitive terms, mainly, I think, under the influence of the highly successful cognitive revolution in psychology in the last 20 years. But more recently it has been shown by Joseph Forgas[15] that when you ask people to classify the social situations that they typically encounter, the categories they use are affective, not cognitive. There are a number of interesting implications following from this, but the one I want to underline is that such categories cut across classification by frames or schemata.

In narrative, if frames or schemata provide an inadequate interpretive matrix for reading, it seems likely that a similar cross-domain process of categorisation will also be taking place during reading. I looked at this possibility in another study, which was modelled loosely on the procedure of Forgas.[16] Forgas's work required him to employ a group of people who knew and understood each other well, and were strongly motivated to do what he was asking. Following his example, I selected a group of students who knew each other well and were interested in the study. They were six third-year education students who volunteered to participate.

I provided these students with a story by Pritchett, called 'Many Are Disappointed',[17] two weeks in advance of the experimental session. The story concerns a party of male cyclists, who arrive at a pub in a remote part of the countryside. The pub turns out not to serve beer. A woman with a small child serves the party with tea. The warmth of the relationship of one of the visitors with the woman and child contrasts with the rather crude and basic expectations of the rest of the party.

From the text of the story I selected 24 episodes which I judged to be a representative selection of the main types of scene and incident in the story. The students began by putting these scenes, which were typed on separate pieces of paper, into six to eight groups in any way they chose according to their understanding of the story. They then discussed among themselves (while I absented myself from the room) ways of comparing and contrasting the scenes, and devised nine rating descriptions that they all agreed they could use. The 24 scenes were then rated on the nine descriptions.

I was interested in seeing what descriptions would be devised. Two were affective: one clearly so, *passionate–detached*, and the other, *subjective–objective*, affective in the less direct sense that subjective usually connotes coloured by affect. The other seven were descriptive of character, action or situation. I compared the free groupings made in the first part of the session within the ratings, to see which descriptions matched the pattern of the free groupings most closely, using a correlation technique. As I had expected, it was the affective descriptions which matched the most closely: the correlations here reached a highly significant level. Of the seven neutral descriptions, six correlated only at a low or non-significant level. Thus when these readers compared and contrasted the 24 scenes of the story in the free groupings at the beginning, it turns out that the categories they were using were predominantly affective ones.

This suggests that in working towards an understanding of how episodes in a story relate, it is the affective implications of the episodes which are the main factor. The affective connections supersede the connections between episodes which are cognitively similar. The affective groupings, in other words, cut across conceptual domains, allowing thematic concerns to develop at the secondary or 'aesthetic' level of meaning. Thus, when the conceptual 'frame' for understanding a particular scene is undermined or fails, the scene is likely to have affective links with scenes in other conceptual domains. In this way an alternative mode of interpretation is opened up, leading to the transformation of the scene and its integration into a higher level of understanding

CONCLUSION: THE SELF AND THE TEXT

The empirical studies I have mentioned concerned only a few students and two stories, and can of course carry little weight on their own. I hope to undertake several similar studies involving a wider range of texts, to see if the evidence for the key role of emotion can be replicated and, if so, to what extent different types of text can be distinguished empirically. At a more theoretical level, the shift of attention to emotion brings into focus several other important issues. I would like to conclude this paper with a brief mention of these. They are the status of the self and the unity of the text.

The interpreting self in recent theory has of course become problematic. We have learnt to be wary of the assumption that the self is autonomous, self-determining, and so forth. As Michaels shows,[18] this view is an inheritance from Descartes, who presupposed a conscious self as an absolute, prior to any knowledge. C. S. Pierce, an objector to this view, argued that we can think only in signs; therefore to think of the self is to think in signs, thus the self is a social construct. Our idea of the self cannot come from direct knowledge or intuition: the self is a construct or inference from our perception of others. The major theory of the self in recent cognitive social psychology has echoed this: the self is mirrored in our interactions with others. There are recent studies in psychology suggesting that this is mistaken: it is knowledge of the self which is primary and such knowledge is constituted primarily in emotional form. Moreover, when we are not concerned simply with the appearance or behaviour of others, we also project this affective, self-referential information onto understanding others.[19] This leads me to dissent from a common account of character in narrative theory.

When we read about characters, how is the information encoded? What is recalled about a character who reappears halfway through a story, or after we have finished reading? It is Seymour Chatman's thesis that what we extract is traits.[20] I suggest it is motives. This allows us to encompass several alternative ways of understanding character, such as actants or traits: motives explain behaviour, that is, what characters do as actants and why; and traits are the relatively enduring style, the how, of what is done. But in the last analysis it is motive which is more important than traits.

In this sense the two senses of motive come together in the reader: characters have motives; events in a narrative and shifts in frame need to be motivated. What is being appealed to in both senses is the reader's own motivational system, and his sense of identity which is bound up in it. My first study pointed to the structural role of the reader's sense of motivation, and a similar finding has been reported before. Motivation turned out to be a significant variable in two studies of response in which high school and freshman responses to novels were studied.[21] Statements of self-involvement correlated with statements indicating literary judgement and evaluation: this suggested that self-involvement was a necessary prerequisite to interpretation.

Thus events in a story need to be 'motivated' in order to be assimilated, and if motives are not self-evident, they must either be supplied by the narrator, or their discovery is the focus of narrative interest. Here the reader's own motivational system will supply the cues for interpretation. Such an approach does not call for a unity of motives in the reader. On the contrary, it is quite possible to envisage that a conflict of motives may underlie a given reading.

The second unity that is postulated is that of the text. The fact that there may exist unity of a certain kind in the text is suggested by the data from the first study. The rank orderings for importance undoubtedly reflected some wide variations in individual judgements. A few phrases received ranks varying across the range from one to six (most important to least important). The cluster analyses, nevertheless, show a high degree of consistency in the grouping of phrases. How is this to be explained? A previous study I did involving the affective structuring of response to literary texts[22] suggested that affective response among readers varies considerably, but that the affective links between different text elements tend to remain constant from one reader to the next. Readers bring their own affect to colour in a structure which is largely determined by the text. Similarly, while readers are making predictions based on the same elements of a story, the affective causes of the predictions may vary. Literary texts thus contain relatively powerful constraints over the structuring of response but not over its affective meaning, which is likely to vary from one reader to another.

Clearly, more study of this aspect of texts is required. Unlike the schema or goal-generated relationships postulated by other methods of text analysis, it exhibits an aspect of text structure which is independent of specific content in the sense that affective meaning appears to vary widely across readers. On the other hand, as the decisive, structuring effect of emotion in response comes from the generation of uncertainty, it can be argued that the ultimate source of the commonality of response lies in the shared knowledge of the frames and conventions which a text then defamiliarises. Such knowledge constitutes what Stanley Fish would call the interpretive community.[23] It is in our affective responses that we begin to diverge as individuals, which points to the diversity of meanings which the same text comes to have among a group of readers – as we know from our seminars with students, or from the pages of the journals. We are a community only in the shared knowledge we bring to the text; in the transforming effects determined by emotion the literary text speaks to us as individuals. And it is, finally, the constructive features of emotion in us as individuals through which we construct our understanding of the text as a whole.

Notes

1. Menakhem Perry, 'Literary Dynamics: How the Order of a Text Creates its Meanings', *Poetics Today*, 1 (1979), 35–61; Wolfgang Iser, *The Act of Reading: A Theory of Aesthetic Response* (London: Routledge & Kegan Paul, 1978).
2. Roman Ingarden, *The Literary Work of Art*, trans. G. Grabowicz (Evanston, Illinois: Northwestern University Press, 1973).
3. Michael Riffaterre, 'Describing Poetic Structures: Two Approaches to Baudelaire's "Les Chats",' in Jane P. Tompkins, ed., *Reader-Response Criticism from Formalism to Post-Structuralism* (Baltimore: Johns Hopkins University Press, 1980); Wolfgang Iser, *The Implied Reader* (Baltimore: Johns Hopkins University Press, 1974); Christine Brooke-Rose, 'The Readerhood of Man', in Susan R. Suleiman and Inge Crosman (eds) *The Reader in the Text: Essays on Audience Interpretation* (New Jersey: Princeton University Press, 1980).
4. For recent statements by Norman Holland and David Bleich see their

papers in Charles R. Cooper, ed., *Researching Response to Literature and the Teaching of Literature* (Norwood, New Jersey: Ablex, 1985).

5. Jonathan Culler, 'Prolegomena to a Theory of Reading', in *The Reader in the Text*, p. 55.
6. Norman Holland, 'Re-Covering "The Purloined Letter": Reading as a Personal Transaction', in *The Reader and Text*, p. 366; *5 Readers Reading*, pp. 247–8.
7. Clare Hanson, *Short Stories & Short Fictions, 1880–1980* (London: Macmillan, 1985).
8. As Seymour Chatman accepts: see *Story and Discourse: Narrative Structure in Fiction and Film* (Ithaca: Cornell University Press, 1978) p. 128.
9. Perry, 'Literary Dynamics'; Iser, *The Act of Reading*, p. 92; Roland Barthes, *S/Z*, trans. Richard Miller (London: Jonathan Cape, 1975), pp. 18–20.
10. Iser, in *Reader-Response*, pp. 62–4, p. 68.
11. Perry, op. cit., p. 37.
12. Rand Spiro, Avon Crismore and Terence Turner, 'On the Role of Pervasive Experiential Coloration in Memory', *Text*, 2 (1982), 253–62.
13. *A Haunted House* (London: Hogarth Press, 1944), *The Common Reader*, First Series (London: Hogarth Press, 1929).
14. For a similar finding, showing that predictions are made by readers of stories but not expository prose, see G. M. Olsen, R. L. Mack and S. A. Duffy, 'Cognitive Aspects of Genre', *Poetics*, 10 (1981), 283–315.
15. Joseph P. Forgas, 'Affective and Emotional Influences on Episode Representations', in J. P. Forgas, ed., *Social Cognition: Perspectives on Everyday Understanding* (London: Academic Press, 1981), 165–80.
16. E.g. Forgas's study of two football teams: see *Social Episodes: The Study of Interaction Routines* (London: Academic Press, 1979), pp. 182–94.
17. V. S. Prichett, *Collected Stories* (London: Chatto & Windus, 1956).
18. Walter Benn Michaels, 'The Interpreter's Self: Pierce on the Cartesian "Subject" ', in *Reader-Response*, pp. 185–200.
19. I examine some of the evidence for this at more length elsewhere: 'Emotion and the Self: The Context of Remembering', *British Journal of Psychology*, 77 (1986), 389–97.
20. Chatman, p. 126.
21. These studies, by James Wilson and James Squire, are described by David Bleich, in *Reader-Response*, pp. 138–40.
22. 'The Structure of Response: A Repertory Grid Study of a Poem', *Research in the Teaching of English*, 19 (1985), 254–68.
23. Stanley Fish, *Is There a Text in This Class? The Authority of Interpretive Communities* (Cambridge, Massachusetts: Harvard University Press, 1980), p. 171.

3

'Things out of Words': Towards a Poetics of Short Fiction[1]

CLARE HANSON

I would like to begin with two descriptions of the act of writing short stories, or fictions.[2] First, Katherine Mansfield, writing, rather incongruously, to Hugh Walpole:

> You know that strange sense of insecurity *at the last*, the feeling 'I know all this. I know more. I know down to the minutest detail and *perhaps more still*, but shall I dare to trust myself to tell all?' It is really why we write, as I see it, that we may arrive at this moment and yet – it is stepping into the air to yield to it – a kind of anguish and rapture.[3]

And Eudora Welty, in 1955:

> The simplest-appearing work may have been brought off (when it does not fail) on the sharp edge of experiment, and it was for this its writer was happy to leave behind him all he knew before, and the safety of that, when he began the new story.[4]

Both writers stress the attraction of the unknown and are complicit with the doubleness this embodies as an image of that which is desired but continually displaced – it is an extreme image of desire which violates the 'natural' relationship of antithesis between absence and presence. Note, too, that Katherine Mansfield writes of 'stepping into the air' – again a kind of underscoring of absence/death – 'anguish' before (and causing?) 'rapture'.

I want in this paper to try to isolate some of the specific qualities and effects of the short story. I would argue strongly that the short story provides or makes for a kind of experience for the reader which is quite different from that which she or he gains from the novel. I think that the difference, too, is one of kind, not of degree. The novel, of course, is the form with which the short story is most often compared – the story is defined 'against' the novel, which is considered to be the major form and the norm in fiction. The short story is often seen as the 'little sister' of the novel – and because it is defined in terms of the novel, it is bound to fail in many respects when it comes up for judgement. The short story is often not so much condemned as bracketed off, because it is considered that it lacks the 'breadth', scope, universality and representative qualities of the novel. Because it is short, the material must be fragmentary, subjective, partial: if the material is fragmentary, subjective, partial and so on, the form must be short – it is a circular argument.

In attempting to pin down some of the general qualities of the short story, I would like first to make an observation. To generalise, is it not the case that in the novel, detail which is stressed and selected for attention will normally lead us back into the text, while detail which is stressed and foregrounded in the short story will tend to lead us out of the text – and part of its meaning then lies in its anomolous nature, its tangentiality? To take an example: perhaps the most vivid (visual) image which remains with us after reading Henry James's *The Portrait of a Lady* is that of Madame Merle and Gilbert Osmond arrested in a moment of at first incompletely understood informality in Chapter 40. I would argue that we cannot seek for the meaning of that image outside the context of the originating text. In James's story 'The Jolly Corner', however, the repeated 'close encounters' of the central figure invite an interpretation which almost by definition must come from outside the immediate context of the text. This 'open' quality of the short story is not simply a condition of the literal brevity of the form. It does *not* occur, that is, because in a short story there is no space for cross-reference or repetition of the kind we are familiar with in the novel. It is rather the result of what Roman Jakobson would call a fundamental difference in the 'set' of the two forms of the short story and novel. Within the novel, images function metonymically, though the novel is not itself metonymic in relation to 'reality'. Each image as it appears resumes something of what has preceded it in the text. In the short story foregrounded details or 'images' tend to resist such interpenetration and integration –

which is why they disturb us in a peculiar, a distinctive and distinctly non-novelistic way.

I would like to take further the idea of a difference in the 'set' or orientation of the forms of the novel and short story. It has been argued by Formalist, Structuralist and Post-structuralist critics alike that any given 'element' – word, detail or image – turns into something else, becomes a 'token of something else', in Borges's suggestive phrase, as it enters into the articulation and organisation of a literary work as a whole. Post-structuralist critics have argued too that any literary work may be characterised as a structure of representation and selection founded on the primary impulse to dream/desire: the greater the orientation towards desire, the further, they argue, language is removed from its functional and restricted meaning. Eudora Welty seems to describe exactly such a process of re-orientation and transformation in a discussion of 'literary' language in *The Eye of the Story*: she describes too the unsettling effect for the author of a state of mind in which words are allowed to move freely, following, to use a rather clumsy figure, their own desire:

> We start from scratch, and words don't; which is the thing that matters – matters over and over again, for though we grow up in the language, when we begin using words to make a piece of fiction, that is of course as different from using even the same words to say hello on the telephone as putting paint on canvas is. This very leap in the dark is exactly what writers write fiction in order to try.[5]

I am working towards the suggestion that the short story is a more 'literary' form than the novel in this sense – in its orientation towards the power words hold, or release and create, over and above their mimetic or explicatory function. Words, as Lacan has argued, may be chosen in any given work of literature for reasons which have as much to do with the movement of unconscious desire as with the production of literal meaning. Lacan argues that desire is continually playing over language, deeply informing its structure. I would suggest that the short story writer in particular *courts* such a play of language: this is a part of what she or he is seeking in the 'unknown', with its 'anguish' and 'rapture'.

In this connection let us return to that 'limited' quality of the story which is often adversely compared with the inclusive, universal power of the novel. The term limited may be interpreted in an unpejorative as well as a pejorative sense, as meaning not only something 'restricted', to stick to the *Oxford English Dictionary* terms, but also something around which 'bounds' have been drawn. If we take the second sense, the word limited may suggest simply the concept of framing, as in a picture. Could one suggest that the tight structure and strict requirements of the short story form act in the widest sense as a frame, or limit, which allows a narrative to remain in a more fragmented but also in a more suggestive state than is possible in the novel? (This is a point which, as we will see, relates to the concept of 'literary' language discussed above, and to the idea of the importance of desire in the short story). The frame acts as an aesthetic device, permitting ellipses (gaps and absences) to remain in a story, which retains a necessary air of completeness and order because of the very existence of the frame. We thus accept a degree of mystery, ellision, uncertainty in the short story as we would not in the novel.

This formal property of the short story may facilitate two things. First, and perhaps most importantly, it can allow images from the unconscious mind to fuel a short story and to present themselves in the text in a relatively *untranslated* state. Such images retain an air of mystery and impenetrability, an air of dream. They exist as much as figures of unconscious desire as consciously representational images. In this respect we should bear in mind the function of the image in relation to the unconscious. In Lacanian thought the image, as a mental/visual manifestation, acts as a metaphor for – a substitute for – a repressed signifier. The subject, that is, cannot admit a given meaning to consciousness, cannot admit it to the conscious world of the Symbolic. The meaning can be expressed, however, through the non-verbal image-token in the world – precisely – of the Imaginary.

The second point about ellision in the short story relates to the movement of desire on the part of the *reader*. The imagination of the reader is stirred in a particular way by the elliptical structure of many short stories. Ellisions and gaps within a text offer a special space for the workings of the reader's imagination, offer space for the work of that image-making faculty which would otherwise lie dormant: the reader's desire is thus allowed, or rather invited, to enter the text. In this connection, we may link desire with fantasy and 'what cannot be, but *is*'.[6] It is not enough in this context to define fantasy simply in terms of a negative or antithetical relation to the real. Fantasy points to things which do/may exist beyond the known real – the fantastic is not just an inversion of reality, that is, but works on the margins of reality, on the 'dangerous edge' of the unknown. We might put it another way by saying that fantasy is sited at a crossing point of desire and absence/death: in entering into fantasy we fear for the (known) self which must 'die' and be reconstituted via fantasy and an extension of imaginative/imaginary possibility.

Having looked very briefly at general characteristics of the short story/short fiction, I would like now to focus on the 'form' which seems to offer the most obvious model or correlate for the short story. The dream draws together many of the characteristics of the short story outlined above – it may indeed be said to consist of the expression of repressed desire via, often, the fantastic. Could one argue that the short story is the narrative art form most closely associated with dream? Eudora Welty writes, referring to an early fantasy story:

> I never wrote another such story as that, but other sorts of vision, dream, illusion, hallucination, obsession and that most wonderful interior vision which is memory, have all gone to make up my stories, to form and to project them, to impel them.[7]

Short story writers as diverse as Kipling and Katherine Mansfield, Hemingway and Elizabeth Bowen, Frank O'Connor and Flannery O'Connor, have written of the importance of dream in fuelling their work, 'forming, projecting and impelling [it]', as Welty puts it. Again, it is not just that short stories may literally have their origin in dreams (as, for example, did Katherine Mansfield's story 'Sun and Moon') – it is more that they may be *structured like dreams*. The short story would seem to be closer in its organisation to dream than to reality in the sense in which we usually employ the term 'reality' in (antithetical?) relation to literature. Could it be that the *structure* of a short story (or dream) is significantly unlike the *grammar* of a novel narrative, which depends on order, incidence and sequence in a way that the short story does not? The temporality of the short story – its extensive physical nature (namely, time taken over reading), its dependence on pacing and conventional 'time-keeping' – is heavily qualified by the fact that 'events' in a good many short stories are not seen primarily as the fruits of time or as the culmination of long processes. They tend to have a random and arbitrary nature, and the relationship which we would expect to find between them is frequently disturbed or violated. One could then argue that events/images in stories/fictions are related rather as they are related in dreams, 'impelled', to use Welty's term again, by unconscious forces, rather than being related in the more 'normal' terms of order and sequence by which we attempt to organise our conscious lives.

If we accept this suggestion for the moment, we may profit from a closer look at the ways in which dreams are structured. The work of Jean-Francois Lyotard, who has revised extensively the Freudian model of the dream, is particularly revealing in connection with the short story and its effects. Lyotard has argued forcibly against Freud's analysis of the structure of dreams – and of the structure of the work of art which Lyotard sees as analogous (he writes 'the "language" of the dream seems to be nothing more nor less than the language of art. It is iis primary cause, perhaps its model').

Lyotard takes issue with Freud's assumption that the dream consists of latent thoughts which are transformed into the manifest dream content through the agency of an active censoring power (that is, through some form of the super-ego). He suggests instead that it is *desire itself* which reworks the dream thoughts to create the dream's manifest content. The crucial point is that this would indicate that we should not attempt to 'read' the dream in a Freudian sense, looking for a significance which lies 'behind' it. Rather we should say that it is the dream itself which *is* latent desire expressed. Hence its extraordinary power, its combination of the elements of familiarity and strangeness, and hence too the need to 'read' the dream not 'symptomatically' but *literally*.

Lyotard's argument for the way in which a dream should be viewed offers an interesting prototype for the way in which we might read short stories. I have been trying throughout this paper to express something of the mysterious but also obdurate nature of the short story, its strangeness *and* its familiarity. Does this combination of strangeness and familiarity derive from the fact that the short story is, more readily and more frequently than the novel, a channel for the expression of repressed or unconscious desire? If this were true, the story would be (for both author and reader) strange in that it is the expression or embodiment of previously unknown and repressed desire and familiar precisely because desire hollows out and is the obverse image of that which is already known, that which already exists.

To summarise the argument so far: we might say in this context that short stories often do not 'tell' us things, despite the semantic proximity of the words story and tale – they 'are' things. To elaborate a little, we might consider the role of the image in the short story. It is a commonplace to say that the visual and spatial image is of central importance in the structure of many short stories and fictions. In classical psychoanalytic theory, as in Lacanian theory, the image is identified with desire (the imaginary). Again, Lyotard extends the classical Freudian model in this context, arguing that the dream (text) may consist of warring forces of the figural and the discursive. He sees desire, embodied in the image, as existing in an adversarial relationship to discourse (narrative) – desire murders, condenses, freezes narrative:

> Now this mobility which manufactures things out of words, is it not desire itself, pursuing its usual course, producing the imaginary? If this is the case, then we should not say that condensation is an exercise by means of which desire disguises itself, but rather that it is *desire working over* the text of the dream-thoughts. In the first of these interpretations, the force is located *behind* the manifest content, itself assumed to be a disguised text; in the second, and apparently correct one, the force, on the contrary, compresses the primary text, crumpling it up, folding it, squabbling the signs it bears on its surface, fabricating new units which are not linguistic signs or graphic entities. The manifest content is the old text 'forced' in this manner; it is not a text. Force occupies the very scenario of the dream as Van Gogh's brush-stroke remains recorded in his suns.[8]

This distinction between narrative – associated with the super-ego and the conscious mind – and image – associated with the id and the unconscious – may clearly have profound implications for psychoanalysis, literary theory and aesthetic theory in general. Lyotard posits a violent hierarchy in which the poised (not static) image has primacy over narrative, discourse, text. While it would be meaningless to suggest that any and all 'images' are expressive of unconscious desire, and while it is clear too that Lyotard is in Derrida's thrall in his mistrust of 'linguistic signs', I think there is an important point here, or a suggestive analogy for our consideration of the particular power of the image-dominated short story form. For Lyotard text is associated with 'old', unregenerate meanings, 'image' with new meaning. Could one suggest that the short story is often committed to the discovery of new meaning in much the way Lyotard indicates, through a strategy of revising and 'condensing' old texts and known meanings? This would account for what I would like to call its 'supra-graphic' quality, in which it would seem to be cognate with the secondary dream manifestation described by Lyotard in the passage quoted above.

I would like if I may briefly to take an example at this point, from the story 'The Blue Hotel' by Stephen Crane. The core meaning of this story seems to lie in the image (in the double, literal and figural senses of the word) of the blue hotel itself. This arises as in a dream, as an object perceived in the mind's eye, coming out of darkness and absence, related to nothing before or since. The image looms over the story, its meaning signally unaffected by the encounters which constitute the apparent 'story' – and this 'unaffected', obdurate quality is what remains with us, fascinating yet baffling, thwarting normal hermeneutic strategies:

> The Palace Hotel at Fort Romper was painted a light blue, a shade that is on the legs of a kind of heron, causing the bird to declare its position against any background. The Palace Hotel, then, was always screaming and howling in a way that made the dazzling winter landscape of Nebraska seem only a grey swampish hush. It stood alone on the prairie, and when the snow was falling the town two hundred yards away was not visible. But when the traveller alighted at the railway station he was obliged to pass the Palace Hotel before he could come upon the company of low clapboard houses which composed Fort Romper, and it was not to be thought that any traveller could pass the Palace Hotel without looking at it. Pat Scully, the proprietor, had proved himself a master of strategy when he chose his paints. It is true that on clear days, when the great transcontinental expresses, long lines of swaying Pullmans, swept through Fort Romper, passengers were overcome at the sight, and the cult that knows the brown-reds and the subdivisions of the dark greens of the East expressed shame, pity, horror, in a laugh. But to the citizens of this prairie town and to the people who would naturally stop there, Pat Scully had performed a feat. With this opulence and splendour, these

> creeds, classes, egotisms, that streamed through Romper on the rails day after day, *they had no colour in common.*[9] [My italics]

(It is not for nothing of course that colour, a visual key, sets the note and gives the tone for other of Crane's stories – 'The Red Badge of Courage', 'The Bride Comes to Yellow Sky').

To return to our opening point: the short story is a form which hugs the unknown to itself. It is a form committed to the unknown, precisely to the *obscure* object of desire. The unknown cannot become known in the expected sense, for that would be to reduce or deny it. If the short story is the narrative form most closely implicated with desire, its content will always remain to an extent in a latent, potential state. And in being so implicated with desire, the short story will also be a very 'literary' form in the sense in which the term is used by Tzvetan Todorov in *The Poetics of Prose* (a text concerned very largely, it may be noted, with the *tales* of Henry James). Todorov writes that

> By speaking of desire it (literature) continues to speak . . . itself.[10] [Todorov's ellipsis]

In this sense the short story is, we might suggest, a more self-referential, more 'literary' form than the novel. This is a feeling, surely, which many short story writers have had, though they may not have analysed it precisely as Todorov has done. Nonetheless, in testifying to the importance of 'language' in the short story, practitioners of the form have pointed to its 'literary' quality, that is, to its self-referential, free-standing linguistic quality which is connected with an orientation towards desire. This 'literary' quality may be felt, ultimately, I think, as some kind of disjunction between reader and text: in contradistinction to the reader of a novel, the reader of a short story cannot easily lapse into the assumption that what she or he is reading about is 'life' (by which she or he means her/himself). Todorov makes this point bluntly:

> The public prefers novels to tales, long books to short texts, not because length is taken as a criterion of value, but because there is no time, in reading a short work, to forget it is only 'literature' and not 'life'.[11]

Another satisfaction is denied us in the short story/short fiction:

if the short work is structured like a dream, its constituent parts being related in ways obscure to reader and writer, then it might be argued that the short work refuses to give us a world of law and order. We are refused a point of entry into and identification with the text and are denied the v(ic)arious satisfactions which we derive from seeing the characters of a novel take action, thus appearing to control the fearful endlessness of reality. The question of sequence and relation in the short story is difficult, however. To what extent can relation be equated with narration in the short story? I have suggested that the short story may often refuse a certain level of narrative, that it is not as it were 'stitched together', as narrative, by the operations of the conscious mind. In the relation of its parts there is a dream quality which refers us back to the operations of the unconscious.

One further point arises. We have argued that in its connection with the unknown and with fantasy the short story is a form which is close to the unconscious. Here lies, perhaps, the source both of its power and its powerlessness – and this may be why it is a form which will, always, remain on the margins of literature.

I would like to finish by referring to a story by Eudora Welty from *The Curtain of Green and Other Stories*. Having quoted the opening of Crane's 'The Blue Hotel' I would like now to consider the conclusion of Welty's story 'Clytie'. I have stressed throughout this paper the 'difference of view' between the short story and the novel: no novel could, I contend, end in quite this way, on such a note of (literally) suspended animation. It is appropriate to conclude perhaps that if, as Todorov suggests, the 'first law' of literature is that 'it remains its own essential object', then it is only the *text* 'Clytie' (not the character Clytie) which can here locate itself as the legitimate object of its own desire:

> Clytie swayed a little and looked into the slightly moving water. She thought she saw a face there.
>
> Of course. It was the face she had been looking for, and from which she had been separated. As if to give a sign, the index finger of a hand lifted to touch the dark cheek.
>
> Clytie leaned closer, as she had leaned down to touch the face of the barber.
>
> It was a wavering, inscrutable face. The brows were drawn together as if in pain. The eyes were large, intent, almost avid,

the nose ugly and discolored as if from weeping, the mouth old and closed from any speech. On either side of the head dark hair hung down in a disreputable and wild fashion. Everything about the face frightened and shocked her with its signs of waiting, of suffering.

For the second time that morning Clytie recoiled, and as she did so, the other recoiled in the same way.

Too late, she recognised the face. She stood there completely sick at heart, as though the poor, half-remembered vision had finally betrayed her.

'Clytie! Clytie! The water! The water!' came Octavia's monumental voice.

Clytie did the only thing she could think of to do. She bent her angular body further, and thrust her head into the barrel, under the water, through its glittering surface into the kind, featureless depth, and held it there.

When Old Lethy found her, she had fallen forward into the barrel, with her poor ladylike black-stockinged legs up-ended and hung apart like a pair of tongs.[12]

Notes

1. Some of the ideas for this paper first found expression in 'Limits and Renewals: the meaning of form in the stories of Rudyard Kipling', an essay for *Kipling Considered*, Phillip Mallett (ed.) (London: Macmillan, 1988). I am particularly grateful to colleagues at the Symposium on the Short Story who pointed me towards areas which needed further work.
2. For the distinction between short stories and short fictions see my *Short Stories and Short Fictions, 1880–1980* (London: Macmillan, 1985). There I suggest that the term 'story' should be reserved for those short narratives in which the major emphasis is on plot: the term 'fiction' might denote those short narratives – usually more recent ones – in which plot is subordinate to psychology and mood.
3. C. K. Stead (ed.) *The Letters and Journals of Katherine Mansfield* (Harmondsworth: Penguin, 1977), p. 189.
4. Eudora Welty, *The Eye of the Story* (New York: Vintage Books, 1979), p. 110.
5. Ibid., p. 134.
6. Rosemary Jackson, *Fantasy* (London: Methuen, 1981) p. 23.
7. Eudora Welty, *One Writer's Beginnings* (Cambridge, Mass. and London: Harvard University Press, 1984), p. 89.
8. Jean-Francois Lyotard, from *Discours, Figure* (Paris: Klincksiek, 1971);

this translation by Mary Lydon, *Oxford Literary Review*, vol. 6, 1983, no. 1, p. 8.

9. Stephen Crane, *The Red Badge of Courage and Other Stories*, ed. with an Introduction by V. S. Pritchett, (Oxford University Press, 1976), pp. 304–5.
10. Tzvetan Todorov, *The Poetics of Prose*, trans. Richard Howard (Oxford: Basil Blackwell, 1977), p. 107.
11. Ibid., p. 143.
12. *The Collected Stories of Eudora Welty* (Harmondsworth: Penguin, 1983), p. 90.

4

Too Short for a Book?

NICOLE WARD JOUVE

'Longtemps je me suis couché de bonne heure'. 'For a long time I have gone to bed early' – eight words only in the first sentence of a book several thousand pages long, Proust's *A la Recherche du Temps Perdu, Remembrance Of Things Past*. How we know, reading that sentence, that we are beginning to read a very long book, and how Proust chose it as the opening of his great work, are among those many mysteries of literature that, thank God, no one is able to elucidate. It is part of the same mysteriousness that each text of fiction that we write should come with a first sentence, or a sentence or rhythm somewhere, that dictates the length the thing is going to be. We know at once whether it will be 5, 20 or 150 pages, and if someone asks, 'can you write a text of such and such a length', something in us knows what kind of a prose to look for. Often the initial or initiating sentence is a spontaneous birth, something that comes and demands to be, alas, not just born but painfully gestated, fed, laboured at. Perhaps this is also true of verse. Valéry used to say that one line may be given: never two.

What concerns me here is length. The length of the story, as a genre, if it is a genre; and its relation to the book, the thing that is got together, printed and sold as a book. I am concerned with the question for reasons of my own. I am in the process of writing two 'long' stories which have nothing to do with each other, come from different parts of me, are in a different prose, and I realise that I may not be able to publish them because each will be thought too short for a book, which each ought to be, and it would be nonsense to publish them together, which would amount to the right number of pages. I have also recently had a volume refused by several publishers in France on the grounds largely that it was odd. The attempt was for a book that would be neither a collection of short stories nor a novel proper. It was made up of three stories totally separated by time, place and style, but connected by theme and an undercurrent of imagery to do with water, all kinds of waters and liquidities. It also had the same name for the central character in the three stories, but it was not necessarily the same person. Some of the readers had very enthusiastic reactions, others evinced puzzlement and a sense of alienation. Of course, I may have missed my target, not got the thing right. But it is a form that holds a fascination for me, that combination of distinct identity (the story and its difference from other stories) and flowing in and out, interpenetration, and some day I shall return to it. So the question of the story and its relation to the book has urgency for me.

I connect the Western development of the short story as an independent genre with that of magazines and reviews in the 19th century, as Poe did, and as Doris Lessing has done recently in a French interview. The short story perfectly fits the space given to fiction written by a number of contributors inside the format of a magazine. Poe argued that it did so better than the serial, which meant cutting up a novel, producing formally artificial units. I am not sure I agree (for reasons I shall develop later, and that are evident today in the vogue of soap operas). Still, Gide had a point when he said that 'the short story is made to be read at once, in one sitting' (a phrase which is being used as the epigraph to a new magazine, *Nouvelles*, made up entirely of short stories in France. Gide may be right as far as the magazine is concerned. But what about a book?

A story, unlike a novel, may be read at one sitting, but is it made with that intention, so that it, alone, will be read at that sitting? (Which is what does happen to the tale in Balzac's 'La Grande Bretèche', or in James's *The Turn of The Screw*). Or is it intended that other stories by the same author (in a collection) or other stories by other authors (in a magazine, or collection such as *Fathers by Daughters*, edited by Ursula Owen for Virago) be read at the same time? And – is it written at one sitting?

From the writer's point of view, the short story has the advantage that it will be done more quickly – though there are some quintessential, particularly intense or poetic stories that take as long to be written as novels: one of my friends, Anne Roche, has just spent two years over a hundred pages that have been shrunk and cut to ten pages, a text called 'Saïs'. But generally speaking, the time of the writing of the short story is easier to adjust to the time of living. If you are a busy woman (man, sometimes), continuously interrupted by household or career duties, then the shorter span of the story will accommodate that fragmentation better. I personally find it so, but I also remember that extremely busy and interrupted women like Mrs Gaskell and Harriet Beecher-Stowe and George Sand wrote very long novels rather than stories . . . More importantly, if you do not have much time to write, and if you write relatively fast, the story will be easier because you will have less occasion to change and move beyond it by the time you have finished it. I speak from experience, since in the last six years or so I have started at least eight volumes, some, collections of stories, some, long stories, others, novels – and have completed none. But I now find that the long stories are those which I still have a chance to finish. For there is a time to write a thing, and you change, and since good writing is that which creates a correspondence between what is happening to you now and form-giving, since it is a way of finding out that you knew things you did not know you knew, then if you make yourself go back to things conceived and begun too long ago, you are resurrecting something no longer appropriate, and destroying some of the potential you have for finding out through writing. The great problem, when you want to write a novel, is to find a form that will have it in itself to accommodate large things, that will be able to take in the future that is not yet but that will be part of the time of the writing, as well as the past. 'Longtemps je me suis couché de bonne heure.' The sentence treads water, it is about habit, repetition, what persists, it plays in years and years which will become the time of the writing. Stretching before and after (but *not* a waste sad time; a meditative, child-like – for children are those normally who go to bed early – familiar and even good one: 'de *bonne* heure'). In this respect, the short story demands less, and if it turns out to have the power of habit or recurrence in it, to embody something that occurs again and again (as I tried to do with one of the stories in *Shades of Grey*, 'The Immaculate Conception', which is about compulsive house-cleaning), then it achieves that through intensity, a truth that hits, that will be remembered for its impact: as does Katherine Mansfield's 'Miss Brill' in its evocativeness of the veil of illusion the old and lonely may weave for themselves and of the cruelty with which the young will tear that veil.

But the problem of the short story today at any rate is that its length does not fit the format of the book. Short stories do not sell, publishers tell you. A young friend who has translated stories by a magnificent French writer who died three years ago, Geneviève Serreau, has had them repeatedly rejected: 'We can only sell stories if they're by people who are already famous'.

Why don't people buy short stories? Or do they? (Grace Paley, for example, recently has been a great success). Is it that when people buy a book, they want a whole? A *thing*. Because the pleasure of having your attention held over time by the same thing, of having to begin and to end once, and once only, is a powerful element in what you expect from a book? Is there a fetishism of the Book as One?

I began *The Thousand and One Nights* this summer. One of the delights they give is that they are too bulky to make a single volume, unless it be printed like the Bible, so you have to say 'them'. They play with multiplicity and refuse to totalise anyway. If you regard the Bible as *The Book*, you would have to say that *The Thousand and One Nights* are *The Stories*, plural, earlier and better than *The Decameron* or *The Canterbury Tales* or Perrault or Grimms' fairy tales or any other Western collection of stories. (I imagine the Chinese must have their stories, too, but have not read them yet.) Their plurality expresses for me what is one of the prime pleasures of the story, that it plays or should play with abundance, with the contrasts and contradictions of life, with high and low, not trying to make a *whole* out of them but letting each exist at its own pace and its own tone, letting each man and woman tell their story in their own words and with their own degree of wit, flamboyance, eloquence or rumbustiousness. They are a 'vivier', a trout-farm, of stories. But also (since what concerns me here is the story and the book, how they hold attention), *The Thousand and One Nights* not only show how multiple stories can co-exist, inter-relate and spawn others inside a vast and infinitely mobile form, one that demands as much or more time in the reading than *La Recherche du Temps Perdu, but* the stories ceaselessly rupture the unit. And so, there is no risk of totalisation, by which I mean the drive to homogenise experience by making what is diverse and specific into a unified whole, which is the overwhelming temptation of the Book. No formal tyranny or terrorism can work though Scheherazade nightly survives the death-threat of an all-powerful monarch.

Remember. King Shahriar, made furious by his wife's multiple infidelities, takes a new, virgin bride every night and has her put to death at dawn. The vizir's elder daughter, Scheherazade, says she can end the devastation. She gets married to the king, but asks that her little sister Donaziade be in the bridal room and as soon as the King has finished with her, should say, 'Tell me one of those wonderful stories that you know'. Scheherazade asks the King's permission, and this being granted, embarks on the first of her many nights. Nightly, in order to gain her reprieve, she has to stop a story mid-way, or just after the beginning or before the end: 'She saw the dawn and, discreet, grew silent'. Her discretion may have to do with her knowledge that night-time is story-telling time, that the time of the story is night (and any kind of hollow moment, a pause in a journey, a stalemated siege), while the time of living, of politics, is day-time. Indeed, the king goes on to his divan where he rules his kingdom, deals out justice, then when the night comes, returns to Scheherazade. So that a space / time, the time of living, the time of reality, separates each night. Story-telling is an alternative to reality. When it starts, reality stops, life is suspended. There is nothing of the confusing western bind to realism here. Proust evidently knew this, starting as he did his long narrative with the many nights at Combray, and the magic lantern in his childhood bedroom casting its variegated glow on the walls and ceilings.

But in *The Thousand and One Nights* no night can correspond to a full story, since interruption is of the essence. A night may hold several short stories, bits of poetry, aphorisms, or one long story may span many nights. And Scheherazade is also discreet in the sense of cunning. She knows that by stopping under pretext of morning she is holding the king in suspense, and that suspense gains her reprieve. Next night, she reprieves the king from his suspense, his wanting to know, 'what next? And then?' And begins a new process of suspense. She tells to save her life, and in many of the stories she tells this same thing keeps happening to other story-tellers who, of course (the overall story-teller is an interested party) always in the end gain their reprieve, for poetic or comical reasons. Sometimes the story is so beautiful it gives immense pleasure to the listener who was going to have you killed, and he is bountiful in exchange (the gift of your life for your gift to me of pleasure). Sometimes, as in the tale of the hunchback and the barber with the seven brothers, the listener is so overwhelmed by the endless supply of stories that he can not take any more, he says, yes, they do make the sum after all. Bargaining is of the essence of story-telling, it is an *exchange*, riddled with analogies.

Story-telling is also playing against Death: your life or your story. Your life for a story. But it is many-coloured and fun and proliferating and gameful, not stern and Northern like the Knight's game of chess with Death on the beach of Bergman's *Seventh Seal*. Not a few of the story-tellers have brushed with death, suffered mutilations. There are one-eyed men, blind men, men with one hand or fingers or toes or ears or noses missing, eunuchs, women who have lost their husbands or their dowries; but they all have robustly survived their various ordeals. The stories are oddly like the tellers, since not a single story appears whole, that is, they all have to be cut in some way by the morning. Their truncated telling *is* what ensures their reprieve: the king will want to know the end, but the end will lead to more, Scheherazade saying, 'this is nothing compared to such and such a story'.[1] But the truncated telling of the stories is also the sign that they have brushed with death. On the other hand, from the moment when you become master or mistress of suspense you are as powerful as the king.

I see in *The Thousand and One Nights* an archetypal model standing behind all stories, collections of stories, story-telling, even when people are least aware of them. It is the power of great texts that they are of relevance even to those who do not know of them. For any writing that is real puts things at play that are deeper and bigger than consciousness, and that continue to exist beneath what historical moments make visible. Of course, I must not underestimate the influence they have had over the West. Robert Hampson, who knows about them, tells me that it is believed that Cervantes had come across them while he was in North Africa. And translations of various kinds had made them widely available in the 18th and 19th centuries: traces of their impact can be found everywhere, probably from Montesquieu and Voltaire and *Rasselas* and Beckford and Southey to Dickens and Conrad and Joyce's 'Araby' in *Dubliners*. Stendhal used to say he wished he could forget so that every year he could have the pleasure of re-reading both *Don Quixote* and *The Thousand and One Nights*.

I fear that we lost (or failed to hang on to) something when we in the West established a tradition of the story as *single*. Even when they belong with each other, as in *The Decameron*, each story still lasts a day, the span of a day corresponds to the time of story-telling.

Units fit time, something mechanical, eventually perhaps marketable, comes into it. Quantity begins to rule instead of potential infinity. The Sienese banks have become established, Pound would tell us. Measures fit, already as in the metric system, ten times ten; the link with the body, with organic rhythms, has been lost, and with it something of the intense and multifarious nature of suspense. Interestingly, it is the *novel* in the West that seems to have inherited something of the suppleness and multiplicity of *The Thousand and One Nights*. No wonder Stendhal mentions *Don Quixote* in the same breath with them. Also heirs to them are the picaresque tradition up to *Pickwick*, or the structures 'modernist' novelists like Conrad and Joyce or post-modernist ones like Marquez, and perhaps Doris Lessing in *Shikasta*, have been creating. In *Don Quixote* the knight keeps coming across shepherds who tell him stories, innkeepers who read to them manuscripts that have been left with them, and there is sometimes the same chinese boxes effect one finds to the hunchback's tale, the same internal relevance between the inserted stories and the overall story one finds so many examples of in *The Thousand and One Nights*. But perhaps those of us who write short stories have much to learn from the internal congruence of such structures, and from the fountain-head, the Oriental book. Certainly, the collections of short stories I most admire are those which make up an *organic* whole, establish correspondences, some secret and some visible, between the stories that make up the volume. And yet they do not totalise. I am thinking in particular of Geneviève Serreau's *Ricercare* and *Dix-huit mètres cubes de silence* as well as of Tillie Olsen's *Tell Me a Riddle* (and, to a lesser extent, Grace Paley). In *Dix-huit mètres cubes de silence*, 18 stories, 18 cubic metres of silence, Geneviève Serreau sets up space, volume, perspective (something like the way in which Dutch genre paintings play with perspective and infinity), speech and silence, the way people try to, and often, not always, fail to communicate with each other, are immured in their lives, language, preoccupation with themselves, relations to objects. There is in those stories a dialogue of speech with silence, of the sayable with the unsayable, that is not unlike the way night-time dialogues with day-time in *The Thousand and One Nights*.

I wonder though: does the dialectic of life and death, day and night, function in the same way for men and for women writers? Is it gendered? It has struck me very much in *The Thousand and One Nights* that in the stories told by mutilated tellers, the – what in our contemporary preoccupation with Freud and Lacan we would call 'symbolical castration' – is different for men and for women: the men are lame, one-eyed or eunuchs; the women have lost a husband, or a dowry. Lack strikes directly at the bodies of the men, it hits women through the money or men that give them access to marriage, that is to social existence. It would be interesting to find out whether that entails further differences, to the kind of stories they tell, for instance. It is true, however, that Scheherazade, whose life (not social position) is directly under threat, is the overall narrator. The overall overall narrator or gatherer of the stories and inventor of Scheherazade is unknown: the stories were written between the 10th and the 16th century so 'he' (one imagines that narrator somehow as male) is multiple, or compound. But one could then say that the stories are both male and female, since at any rate the overall overall narrator *needs* Scheherazade and her position in relation to the king for the stories to be told. But I ask the question because reading Colette I have been struck by the way she subverts patterns. She wrote a number of longish short stories, or very short novels, which she called her 'whites'. Her 'blacks', she said, were the novels, novels about love (from *Chéri* onwards, novels written in the third person). But the 'whites' are supposedly autobiographical, narrated in the first person by somebody called Colette or Madame Colette. They are in effect a complex mixture of fiction and autobiography corresponding to periods in which, the narrator says, she was not in love so nothing was happening to her. Often they are about what you can as reader only guess at, about being mistaken, and wavering, in your interpretation of people, in the kind of identification you seek with others, about gender, evil and good. The stories also subvert night and day (as well as subvert normative notions of fiction and autobiography, black and white, male and female).

'Rainy Moon' in the story of that name is a day-time phenomenon, a little rainbow globe of light diffracted by a defect in the window-pane onto the wall-paper of a flat which the narrator visits, where she brings copy to a typist, and which turns out to be the very flat where she waited and suffered a number of years before after the break-up of her marriage: in her old bedroom, the typist's young sister waits and seems to suffer, also longing for a lost husband . . . The story turns out to be about magic, beneficent white magic like rainy moon, but also black magic since in effect the young sister is weaving a spell to kill her husband, and succeeds by the end of the story. It ends with a seventh full moon, and the narrator throwing away the text she had been bringing to the typist: what kind of magic is writing, black or white?

There is, in 'Rainy Moon', a redistribution and a spreading of the parts to be found in *The Thousand and One Nights*. Madame Colette is the Author, in a position of power, visiting the sisters, making a story out of their lives, trying to get at Délia's, the younger sister's, secret: she is the Sultan. She is also a teller, in that she is trying to interpret; and Délia is her alter ego, an image of her younger self, who holds her in suspense, for not only is she attracted to her, but Délia makes it clear that what she is weaving, the thing she is making inside her head (which turns out to be the spell that kills her husand) is as hard to make as a book, and very like it. Délia is a rival teller, a possible mirror image. But there is also ambiguity as to whose life is at stake. Maybe it is Délia who is the Sultan? For Madame Colette is in the position of the threatened husband: she is attracted to Délia, sexually, and as to a child: she penetrates the recesses of her bedroom as Prince Charming might enter into Sleeping Beauty's chamber. And at least once, a spell that had been prepared for the husband almost gets her. Does she destroy the text she'd been writing because there has been no reprieve? But though suspense and power, like night and day, black and white, the parts of listener and of narrator, are redistributed in that story, it yet captures something of the multiplicity that is in the Oriental tales. For white is magical, white is seven colours, the spectrum of the rainbow, interpretation shifts endlessly as you read and re-read . . .

Quite appropriately I hope, I have been using *The Thousand and One Nights* for a multiplicity of purposes. To suggest how story-writers could learn from their ways of making the many into a whole that is yet many, and how some have done so; to show how a woman writer can redistribute the gendered or power parts that are in their telling, and yet retain some of their multiplicity. I want to finish by celebrating the way they themselves could be used to shake some modernist assumptions.

Joy, reached in telling and listening as well as in love-making, and reached to its 'extreme limit', repeatedly, is central to the stories. Excess, a lack of the Western taboos on sexual representation and the voyeurism that goes with the transgression of those taboos, are ingrained in them. They seem to provide that 'jouissance' which Barthes was seeking from the *modernist* text – and this, despite the fact that as narrative they are the reverse of modernist, they are *stories*. They also seem to me to be the Devil's or a genie's gift to Bataille. He celebrated eroticism (in *L'Erotisme*) because it partook of the nature of the Gift which had been described by anthropologist Marcel Mauss in his famous essay. Eroticism should be excess, should be gratuitous, celebratory, the drinking of champagne at a feast. Since the exchange of women which Lévi-Strauss had shown to be a cornerstone of 'culture' in *The Elementary Structures of Kinship* had first been used by man to assert his humanity, renounce the satisfaction of the only instinct that can be deferred in order for him to enter into exchange and communication with others, just so now, a further turn of the screw, eroticism should rupture the established taboos to gain access to a new form of humanity, or freedom. Implicit in Bataille as well as explicit in effect if not theory in Lévi-Strauss is the position of women as objects of exchange: for Bataille, an excessive gift, champagne to be drunk at a feast. And that position seems to me to remain that even when, as in the Histoire de l'Oeil, the girl (one of the girls) initiates some of the erotic ventures. By contrast, I find it fascinating (and it goes against my stereotypical notions of Arab culture) that so many of those who *do* the exchanging in *The Thousand and One Nights,* from Scheherazade onwards, should be women. That joy, freedom, excess, should also be the portion of the listener, the listener to poetry as to a funny story: that it should not be hooked on death, sacrifice, transgression, sulphur. Pity nobody took that one up with Bataille.

Pity nobody said, 'It's not *the* Story nor the *History* of *the* eye we want, Monsieur Bataille. It is stories. And most people tend to have two eyes, Monsieur Bataille. And if you've lost one, as the three one-eyed men have in *The Thousand and One Nights,* at least they don't mind that much, and they have wonderful stories to tell. In exchange. The stories of themselves. Not an exchanging of their women. Let us have some more such stories. Let us not make *the* story tend to the dangerous Oneness of the Book'.

Notes

1. Comparatives, unlike superlatives, open up on infinity. When you say, 'the greatest', you are introducing closure. But when you say, as Scheherazade does, 'Ah, but what is hearing the language of men to hearing the language of animals?', you are opening a door on to a multiplicity of new stories.

5

Time and the Short Story

JEAN PICKERING

To the reading of fiction, we bring a frame of reference formed in part by our previous experience of literature. Some of our expectations are conditioned by whether what lies before us is a novel or a short story. If time or energy is limited, we may put a novel aside for an occasion when we can make a greater commitment: three days to *War and Peace*, 24 hours to *Ulysses*, two days to *The Golden Notebook* – although it was decades ago, the time I spent with them remains a block in my memory. I remember the process of reading and the succession of emotional states I went through. In each case, although life outside the novel was reduced to a minimum, it still went on. I ate, showered, fed the baby, and, except in the case of *Ulysses*, slept. My memory of the experience of reading these novels includes a sense of duration.

When we pick up a magazine or a book of short stories, however, we understand that we face a structure we must enter quickly and leave soon. Nevertheless a story may remain with us just as powerfully as a novel. Robert Penn Warren's 'Blackberry Winter', Katherine Anne Porter's 'The Grave', or Margaret Laurence's 'Godman's Master' are clear enough in my mind although I do not remember the actual experience of reading them 30 years ago. The short story is short enough to possess completely; we may recollect it, like a poem, in tranquillity, but only under the most extraordinary circumstances, such as those posited in the movie *Fahrenheit 451*, can we imagine possessing a whole novel. We can possess a short story so completely that the experience of reading may be less significant in our assessment of it than our reflections on it afterwards. Thus, for the reader the relationship of time to the short story is very different from the relationship of time to the novel.

The same is true for the writer. Katherine Mansfield wrote 'The Daughters of the Late Colonel' in a single evening; even fired up by tuberculosis, D. H. Lawrence took six weeks to write *Kangaroo*;

Christiane Rochefort spent 24 days on *A Rose for Morrison*, while Jack Kerouac claimed to have written *On the Road* in three weeks. These facts, of course, say nothing about how long the ideas cooked, simmered (to use Doris Lessing's words), but nonetheless only a certain amount of prior consideration reduces the time spent in composition. Pulp Press International of Vancouver, BC, holds an annual three day competition (novels must be written during the Labor Day weekend) but even the speediest writer cannot produce an entire novel at a single sitting. The rhythms of daily life not only intervene between the intention and the composition, but go on more or less simultaneously with the writing, for even if, like Rochefort, you have a cooperative friend to take care of the housework, cooking, and shopping, or, like Kerouac, someone to roll your joints, nonetheless you have to eat, sleep, and smoke for yourself. Thus in the writer's experience of the two forms, as in the reader's, the relationship to time is a crucial factor.

Although many writers produce both stories and novels, it is rare for anyone to be equally successful in the two forms: D. H. Lawrence and Doris Lessing are prominent exceptions. V. S. Pritchett, William Sansom, and Eudora Welty, for example, have written novels, but clearly they are primarily short story writers; just as clearly, Iris Murdoch, Anthony Burgess, and Margaret Drabble are primarily novelists. In his introduction to the first series of Paris Review interviews, *Writers at Work*, Malcolm Cowley noted that 'among the authors interviewed, the division that goes deepest is not between older and younger writers, or men and women writers, or French and English writers; it is the division between those who think in terms of the short story and those who are essentially novelists' (p. 12). V. S. Pritchett's description of his own attempts to write novels bears out Cowley's observation:

> When I wanted to write short stories and the publisher said he would not publish them unless I would write a novel, I was appalled because I had no idea how to construct a novel. So I read dozens of novels to see how you wrote a novel and I got more and more confused. I did manage to write one slightly anecdotal story which was superficially, shall we say, the plan for a novel which I managed to turn into an apparent novel, but after that I was beginning to write novels in order to please this publisher, and ones which were certainly quite well written but

they had no success. I found that really: short stories were much better.[1]

Pritchett's 'fundamental view about the short story is that it begins as a poetic insight, and . . . is . . . a way of seeing through a situation.'[2] This insight is typically immediate and, as John Wain points out, the decision to use it as a short story is instantaneous: 'Between thinking [that it sounded like an idea for a short story] and making a decision was a microsecond.'[3] This determination of form seems to predate conscious decision. Unlike the instantaneous insight constituting the germ of the short story, the idea for a novel seems to come as a sense of unease, of shifting balance, that can be righted only by full exposition and discovery. Margaret Drabble says that her novels 'seem to grow out of a set of related ideas. If they relate themselves enough, they turn into a novel. I very rarely begin with a character, with a predicament more.'[4] There is a sense of exploration that may be at bottom a personal search: Erica Jong says 'there is something about the *process* of writing a novel that is incredibly revealing about one's own motivations. It's a kind of mediation, a tremendous revelation of self. I don't think I could live without writing novels any more; it's become an inner need.'[5] Writing a novel seems to involve a kind of personal growth. In her introduction to the second edition of *The Golden Notebook*, Doris Lessing describes what she learned while she was writing the novel: 'Perhaps giving oneself a tight structure, making limitations for oneself, squeezes out new substance where you least expect it. All sorts of ideas and experiences I didn't recognize as mine emerged when writing. The actual time of writing, then, and not only the experiences that had gone into the writing, was really traumatic: it changed me' (p. x). These observations by practising novelists emphasise the sense of the novel as process, as gradual discovery rather than instantaneous perception.

There is a further point about the writer's relation to the novel that bears on the present discussion. The writer's memory of the text already completed may be less accurate than a reader's. One has to make so many choices of alternative situations, of details, that a writer may remember the range of options rather than the final choice. It is a common observation that the novel gives more scope for digression and exploration of side issues. All this means that the writer may in fact be able to exert better control over a short story: it can remain in the mind as a single unit, 'the fruit of a single moment of time, of a single incident, or a single perception', as Walter Allen puts it.[6]

Discussions of time in fiction are difficult in part because there is no adequate vocabulary: in this context Susan Sontag complained in 1964 that 'what we don't yet have is a poetics of the novel, any clear notion of the forms of narration'. We are still struggling along without one. Our words for time, particularly those dealing with form in time like shape and pattern, have spatial connotations. This means that we critic-readers tend to minimise the process of reading, the accumulation of expectation, disappointment, sentiment, affection and amusement that reading entails. We downplay the becoming and emphasise the being as though the novel exists all at once like the past, present and future in the mind of a medieval God. This comes about in part because of what Sontag calls 'the habit of approaching works of art in order to interpret them', which emphasises content or statement rather than process. The fact that we can flip back and forth in a book to remind ourselves of what went on at various points where our memory is vague exacerbates this tendency. But neither for the common reader nor for the writer, in particular, does the notion of picture overwhelm the sensation of process. I want to stress this point because the act of doing literary criticism on a novel makes it seem more static, in this respect more like a short story, than it seems to the writer or to the common reader.

What are the implications of the short story's particular relation to time? Here John Gerlach comes to our aid: the short story 'does not condense a longer tale or a longer time period into a short telling. [It] highlights an incident small and slight in itself, presenting it so that the reader must imagine a much larger context. The incident selected would be so deepened by implied extensions as to suggest both the past and the future.'[7] The incident is understood to be symbolic in a general way: it may, as V. S. Pritchett says, crystallise the moment where 'the inner life exposes itself unguardedly.'[8] In short, this instant of revelation is a metaphor for the whole life, a snapshot taken at a representative moment. Thus the short story tends to deal with the unchanging elements of character and emphasises the stability of the essential self, its manner of conception affecting theme as well as structure. In this context it is interesting to note the numbers of short stories that focus on death; in *The Best American Short Stories 1984*, for instance, 11 out of 20 used a death as a central event. It seems that the short story, emphasising stasis as opposed to process, lends itself to depicting death, that moment that fixes human beings, removing us from time altogether.

The novel, on the other hand, emphasises change through time. Time, says Hillis Miller,

> . . . is the main dimension [of the novel] not because it represents the 'stream of consciousness' the 'flux of experience' or 'life as a process' which are essentially spatial terms, implying that time is a linear sequence, a preexistent road or river, but because novels excell in expressing the temporality of the present as a reaching towards the future which will contain a reassimilation of the past. In various ways it represents human existence as standing outside itself, as reaching toward an as yet unprepossessed totality which will complete it. . . . This 'standing outside itself,' this 'reaching toward' are basic characteristics of human temporality.[9]

This narration of the life in time is, as Miller's description of 'human temporality' suggests, closely connected to the principle of causality, the emphasis on which E. M. Forster identifies as the chief constituent of plot in the novel; it uses 'past experience as the cause of present action', as Ian Watt puts it, showing 'a causal connection operating through time'. Indeed a writer who questions 20th-century Western concepts of time and of cause and effect may on that account alone have to reject the novel altogether. Borges, who denied 'the existence of one time, in which all events are linked together',[10] turned to the short story because it is 'less closely involved, structurally and thematically, with the processes of time and with the relations of cause and effect'.[11] H. E. Bates's observations on the art of Stephen Crane, which admirably describe the principle of coherence in the short story in general, emphasise the way in which its structure typically ignores causality: 'The method by which the story is told is not by the carefully engineered plot but by the implication of certain isolated incidents, by the capture and arrangement of casual episodic movements. It is the method by which the surface, however seemingly trivial or unimportant, is interpreted in such a way as to interpret the individual emotional life below.'[12]

The round table discussion on the short story at the Université d'Angers in 1983 came up with the term *revelation* to describe the essential nature of the short story and *evolution* for the novel. The difference can perhaps be put in better focus by a consideration of conclusions. Gerlach says 'the short story is that genre in which the anticipation of the ending is always present'[13]; because the story's relation to the life of the character is essentially metaphoric, implying a future as well as a past for most even if not for Francis Macomber, the story can simply stop. But, says E. M. Forster, 'Nearly all novels are feeble at the end. If it was not for death and marriage I do not know how the average novelist would conclude.' Since 1928 there have been some ingenious ways to avoid these typical plot endings: Woolf brings *Orlando* up to the present moment; echoing *Mrs Dalloway*, Drabble ends *The Middle Ground* by leaving Kate just as her party is about to begin; Lessing returns us to the beginning of *The Golden Notebook* much as Joyce did *Finnegan's Wake*, while she takes *The Four-Gated City* into the future. All these endings stress the continuity, the on-going process of life, the life in time, just as did George Eliot when she closed *Middlemarch* with a lament at leaving her characters: 'For the fragment of life, however typical, is not the sample of an even web.'[14]

Clearly then, the difference in the relations of the two forms to time which first shows in the ways the short story writer and the novelist conceive their subjects – the words *revelation* and *evolution* describe these ways quite as much as they describe the short stories and novels – is manifest in their structures. (This is obviously a spatial word, but the narrow associations *plot* has acquired during its long history render it useless in this context.) Indeed, it is in the structures that readers first notice the different relations to time, which, because it is 'the great invisible in our midst' we can know only by its effects. Although first manifest in the structures, the effects of the different relations to time do not end there. We have already seen that the short story's special relation to time influences theme. It also has profound implications for characterisation.

Scholes and Kellogg hypothesise that characterisation by evolution (what they call '*chronological*, in which the character's personal traits are ramified so as to make more significant the gradual shifts worked in the character during a plot which has a temporal basis [)] . . . is perhaps the principal distinguishing feature of the novel'.[15] Forster's celebrated distinction between flat and round characters is based on precisely this assumption about the nature of characterisation. Because his distinction depends on development over time, his criteria simply do not work for the short story. Flatness depends on repetition, roundness on modification through evolution; these terms are applicable only to characters developing over time, whose contexts are gradually established by the novelists. In a short story, readers must grasp the nature of characters in a moment of revelation; we are called on to supply much of their context either through imagination or experience.

As John Wain has pointed out,

> If you write a short story you can – because you don't need so much detail and because a short story takes one instance of that person's life, takes one specimen moment – you can . . . go and spend a day visiting a factory, you can look at someone working at a factory bench, and you can get a flash of what it must be like to be him or her, and then you can write a short story which gives just one flash of that person. You might get it wrong; it might be a flash that's quite misleading, but assuming that you are going to get it right, you don't need a lot of detail. You could observe that person from the outside, and, therefore, whereas I have written novels, I have always written about the same milieu that I actually live in, and when I've written short stories, I've written about agricultural workers, industrial workers, very old people, children, a boy who was a lifeguard on a bathing beach: things that are not within my ordinary experience, and obviously observed to some extent from outside. . . . But writing a novel about them is not just a matter of sympathizing with them; it is a matter of moving around enormous amounts of information. Now a short story does not need enormous amounts of information.[16]

Thus, unlike novelists who, the old maxim goes, must know everything about their characters, short story writers need only enough details to suggest the main outlines, indeed, if they know more, must rigorously select. The need to present only the essential, permanent features of a character in a characteristic moment means that context in a short story depends to a large extent on what the reader can supply. Typically it is evoked through various kinds of suggestion, such as allusion or metaphor. The short story therefore tends to be doubly symbolic, first in its relation to time with the central event representing the whole life, and second in its delineation of character. A number of well-known short stories characterise through symbol, Lawrence's 'The Captain's Doll' for instance, or Steinbeck's 'Chrysanthemums', or Joyce's 'Araby' with its multiform chalice, or Joyce Carol Oates's 'Mutilated Woman' with her cancerous breast.

Psychoanalysis and the dissemination of Freudian principles throughout Western culture have encouraged the symbolic mode (most obvious in their influence on fictional content, which does not need to be laboured here). It is no coincidence that the short story as we know it and Freud arrived on the scene at approximately the same time. Psychoanalysis has left its mark on structure as well as content: the revelation of the short story is much like the revelation of the analysand. That moment when the sufferer perceives the cause of his suffering, when he undergoes a rebirth into knowledge, becomes a metaphor for the whole life. Classical psychoanalysis has made us into characters with only one story, where all the important events have taken place in infancy, to be repeated throughout life in infinite variations.

These observations make it sound as though structure, content and language can be separated, which does not make much philosophical or critical sense; however, the writer, unlike the reader, experiences the idea of a short story separately from the language it is written in. The idea comes, though it may come attended by point of view and voice; it is given, whereas words are chosen. This initial perception of the appropriate form may determine not only structure and characterisation but even language. A. S. Byatt voices the old maxim that 'Language tries to capture and make permanent a moment in time which won't be captured'.[17] It seems to me that the language of the short story is an extreme case. I will try to explain what I mean by considering the effects of substituting visual images for some part of the narrative: I mean what happens to a short story or novel when it is made into a film. A number of successful films have been made from novels. The BBC versions of *Pride and Prejudice, Brideshead Revisited or Claudius,* for example, did no major violence to the novels from which they were made. In general, short stories translated into film seem to lose a whole dimension. The film pulls against the nature of the short story, which is essentially towards stasis. If there were a good film equivalent for a short story such as the film is to the novel, I would suggest a photograph, and a posed portrait at that, even if it pretended to be a snapshot. The usefulness of this image has not been lost on short story writers: Lionel Trilling's 'Of That Time, of That Place' uses photographs as a way of recording character and Ruth Suckow's 'Four Generations' successfully uses a family portrait as a structuring metaphor much as Joyce uses the chalice and Oates uses the carcinoma. However, I am not offering 'photo is to short story as film is to novel' as an exact equation: the short story loses more in the translation to film than the novel does. Providing visual equivalents for the words of a short story ties them too tightly to the literal referent so that the resonance William Sansom sees as necessary for the short story[18] is stilled, the larger context of metaphorical extensions within which it exists cut away, and the story diminished.

Structure, theme, characterisation, language – all the elements of the short story are influenced by its particular relation to time. Heather McClave maintains that this relation determines the essence of the form. 'The short story . . . embodies the completed moment: immediate, self-contained, isolated from a causal chain of events – much like the modern image of consciousness itself'.[19] We are now less certain of rationality, more tentative of the principle of cause and effect; less sure that science, whether physical or social, can lead us into a better world; more suspicious of linearity, even – although writers cannot afford to indulge in too many doubts about their medium regardless of how many they entertain about the nature of existence – of language itself. The moment of revelation that stands at the heart of the short story, that moment of insight that comes before language, constitutes a discrete moment of certainty in a nebulous universe.

Notes

1. Ben Forkner and Philippe Sejourne, 'An Interview with V. S. Pritchett', *Journal of the Short Story in English*, vol. 6 (1986) p. 25.
2. Ibid., p. 23.
3. John Wain, 'Remarks on the Short Story', *Les Cahiers de la Nouvelle: Journal of the Short Story in English*, vol. 2 (1984) p. 73.
4. Gillian Parker and Janet Todd, 'Margaret Drabble', *Women Writers Talking*, ed. Janet Todd (New York: Holmes and Meier, 1983) p. 168.
5. Wendy Martin, 'Erica Jong', *Women Writers Talking*, p. 24.
6. Walter Allen, *The Short Story in English* (Oxford: The Clarendon Press, 1981) p. 7.
7. John Gerlach, *Towards the End* (University of Alabama Press, 1985) p. 108.

8. V. S. Pritchett, quoted in Clare Hanson, *Short Stories and Short Fictions, 1880–1980* (London: Macmillan, 1985) p. 113.
9. J. Hillis Miller, *The Form of Victorian Fiction* (Cleveland, Ohio: Arete Press, 1979) pp. 14–15.
10. Jorge Luis Borges, 'New Refutation of Time', *Other Inquisitions 1937–1952*, trans. Ruth L. C. Simms (New York: Simon and Schuster, 1965) p. 176.
11. Clare Hanson, *Short Stories and Short Fictions, 1880–1980*, p. 154.
12. H. E. Bates, *The Modern Short Story: A Critical Survey* (London, Michael Joseph, 1972), p. 262.
13. John Gerlach, *Towards the End*, p. 160.
14. George Eliot, *Middlemarch* (Harmondsworth: Penguin, 1965) p. 890.
15. Robert Scholes and Robert Kellogg, *The Nature of Narrative* (Oxford University Press, 1966) p. 169.
16. John Wain, 'Remarks on the Short Story', pp. 52–3.
17. Dusinberre, Janet, 'A. S. Byatt', in *Women Writers Talking*', p. 185.
18. V. S. Pritchett, with William Sansom and Francis King, 'The Short Story', *London Magazine*' no. 6 (1966) p. 12.
19. Heather McClave, ed., *Women Writers of the Short Story* (Englewood Cliffs, N.J.: Prentice-Hall, 1980) p. 2.

6

Gender and Genre

MARY EAGLETON

I have to begin with two disclaimers. Firstly, I am not speaking as an expert on the short story. My aim is to provide some introductory remarks about the relationship between gender and genre in the hope that short story afficionados can extrapolate and develop their own particular connections.[1] I am speaking from my interest in feminist literary criticism, but here lies my second disclaimer, for feminist criticism which has had so much to say about women writers, about literary production, about questions of style, about the construction of meaning, has had much less to say about genre. The silence is not total: the difficulty for women writers to gain access to the major genres has been the subject of critical discussion. Equally, with the development of cultural studies, there has been a growing interest in popular female forms such as romance fiction, or women's rewritings of male-dominated forms – the detective story or science fiction.[2] But at the moment much of the work lacks detail and specificity. Even that most obvious of research areas – women's place in the development of the novel – is only now beginning to get the close analysis it deserves. As late as 1986 Jane Spencer could introduce her study of this very issue with the words:

> Eighteenth-century England witnessed two remarkable and interconnected literary events: the emergence of the novel and the establishment of the professional woman writer. The first of these has been extensively documented and debated, while the second has been largely ignored.[3]

Repeatedly in the criticism I discover useful but undeveloped hints as to how gender and genre might interrelate. The situation is reminiscent of Alice's problem with the Cheshire Cat. When the Cheshire Cat appears it tends to be in unconnected bits, and every time Alice thinks she is getting a clear picture he starts to fade.

Sadly my aim in this talk is not to paint the complete picture but, more modestly, to demarcate some of the main areas in feminism's analysis of genre; then to look more closely at the particular link between women and fiction – my reference here is primarily to the novel but I believe connections can be made with the short story; and finally to consider some theoretical problems which seem to be endemic in feminist criticism and which are certainly important to a feminist consideration of genre.

GENRE AND SEXUAL DIFFERENCE

Feminist criticism's primary response to genre has been to look at it in terms of sexual difference, to try to account for the presence or absence of women in the major genres of the novel, poetry and drama, and to explore further those forms in which women writers are highly represented. As always a good example to begin with is Virginia Woolf. She noticed in *A Room of One's Own* that women writers have been, predominantly, novelists, that significantly fewer have written poetry – 'the original impulse was to poetry', Virginia Woolf declares, but later admits that 'it is the poetry that is still denied outlet' – and that women who aspire to the theatre, if we are to be guided by Judith Shakespeare's biography, are likely to meet a sorry end.[4] For reasons which I shall consider later the novel became a possible form for women. Both poetry and drama have been more problematic. We can look to no single determinant, nor even a convenient handful of such, to explain the discrepancy. A myriad of material and ideological factors – the conditions of production, changes in the publishing industry, critical responses, the gender associations of particular forms – interact in complex and shifting ways influenced by history and culture.

For example, 19th-century criticism seemed to offer the female *lyric* poet a cautious acceptance. If the woman was duly circumspect in the range of emotions that she expressed in her poetry – no lyrics on lust – then her voice of personal feeling and sensitivity could conform with the dominant sexual ideology. In other contexts, however, the personal female voice could be highly disconcerting. A contemporary review of *Aurora Leigh* firmly warns the reader:

> She tells us her own story in the first person singular, and though never woman thought more highly of herself, nor was at more pains to describe her supereminent gifts, she is a very ridiculous person, and what is worse than ridiculous, she is intolerably tedious.[5]

Here the personal voice, because it is declamatory, confident and questioning, becomes objectionable, becomes unfeminine. The female voice that is not involved in gentle introspection but is addressing public issues is intervening in the male arena. In adopting the epic rather than the lyric Elizabeth Barrett Browning crosses the divide from the micro to the macro, from private and domestic to public and social, from feeling to action; in short her choice of form is a radical interrogation of sexual difference. But this is not to argue simplistically that only the epic was contentious and that the lyric remained an unambiguous and socially sanctioned form for women. Nineteenth-century criticism continued to quibble at any lyrical introspection that appeared too self-absorbed. A commitment by the female lyricist to herself or her art could be interpreted as dangerously assertive or egotistic; to focus on Nature, God, or a loved one offered safer material.[6]

In the area of sexual difference, feminist criticism has also drawn attention to the tendency in literary history to privilege the male-dominated forms. High tragedy, epic poetry, sermons, the philosophical treatise, criticism carry more kudos than journals, letters, diaries, even, for the most part, fiction – forms in which women have proliferated. The female forms, we have been told, are less literary, less intellectual, less wide-ranging, less profound. Feminist criticism has insisted that such prioritising does not happen by chance, that generic divisions are not neutral and impartial classifications, and that our aesthetic judgements are ideologically bound. Feminist criticism has been eager to rediscover the hidden women, like Dorothy Wordsworth or Alice James, who wrote their journals and diaries while their male relatives were producing 'great literature'. Too frequently this has led to an invidious competition: is Dorothy's journal really as good as *The Prelude*; would not Alice be as big a name as Henry if only. . . ? But to focus on the women's work questions the prioritising of genres, the definition of 'literature'; it rescues the women's work from being secondary source material, merely an interesting gloss on the primary male text; it raises again the matter of women's restricted access to literary production, how they have turned so often to private forms never intended for public consumption; and it allows the female voice to speak its owner's own experience.

GENRE AND SUBVERSIVE FORMS

The second major way in which feminist criticism has approached the gender/genre debate has been in relating to genre what it sees as the subversive potential of women's writing. There is interest in how women may transform the male-dominated forms and in so doing expose their gender bias. Female appropriations of the Bildungsroman, for example, make apparent what was previously unseen – namely, that these books offer an imaginative construct that is almost entirely male-centred. How radical are these appropriations? Feminist criticism tends to be divided between those who see the shift from hero to heroine as an important political move, and those who doubt whether a change of personnel alters fundamentally the aesthetic and social values of the form. Is a tale of female achievement and individualism a significant enough advance on one of male achievement and individualism?[7] What some critics find more subversive is feminism's questioning of realist forms of writing. To query the truth, coherence and resolution of realism is to undermine the symbolic order. Non-realist forms permit the woman writer to express the contradictions, fantasies or desires that the demands of realism silence. It is in this context that we can understand the involvement of feminist criticism in modernist or avant-garde forms of writing which challenge, in Dorothy Richardson's words, 'current masculine realism'[8]; we can appreciate the renewed concern with utopian writing, with science-fiction, and with what Ellen Moers terms the 'female Gothic'.[9] Above all, we have seen in France the production of a writing that not only disputes realism but which dramatically breaks down all our generic classifications. 'L'écriture féminine' is by turns poetry, philosophy, literary criticism, autobiography, utopian fantasy – and more.

One literary form that has intrigued feminist criticism in recent years, both in terms of sexual difference and in terms of subversive meanings, is popular romantic fiction. The nature of its literary production and consumption, and the analysis of the ideology of romance are the two areas that critics have most readily related to notions of sexual difference. The form is produced, almost exclusively, by women, for women, and about women, though, significantly, the publishing and marketing industries are predominantly in the hands of men. Feminist readership studies have presented the audience as a kind of female sub-culture, the women constructing in their readings their own range of meanings.[10] The ideology of romance has provided an almost classic case-study of sexual difference. We are all familiar with the quintessential romantic hero, dark, brooding and masterful, and the romantic heroine, tremulous, subordinate and focused with doe-eyed adulation on the male. But it is initially difficult to see how the conservative values of Harlequin or Mills & Boon fiction can offer any subversive potential; for example, the resolution of these works lies always in monogamous marital bliss between two white, upwardly-mobile heterosexuals. It has been the application of psychoanalytical theory to the examination of romantic fiction that has led to new understandings. From this perspective romantic fiction is more a sign of women's dissatisfaction with their social lot, of their unfulfilled desires, than a confirmation of their passive anti-feminism. Feminist psychoanalytical theory finds subversive potential in the compulsive and pleasurable aspects of romantic fiction. As Alison Light comments, these stories are 'fantasies . . . the explorations and productions of desires which may be in excess of the socially possible or acceptable'.[11] The disruptive aspect is in the concept of 'excess', of a female sexuality that cannot be represented or fulfilled, but which, equally, cannot be totally silenced.

WOMEN AND FICTION

To return to Virginia Woolf in *A Room of One's Own*. Surveying several shelves of works by women she asks, 'But why . . . were they, with very few exceptions, all novels?[12] Virginia Woolf's response, to look for answers in the social history of women and in the cultural position of the novel, laid the groundwork for future commentaries. The essential pre-condition was the development of capitalism and the move towards industrialisation and urbanisation, which denied middle-class women their traditional occupations. Brewing, baking, spinning, weaving, for instance, which had previously been domestic industries for women, became factory-based industries for men. The aspiration was that the middle-class woman should become a lady of leisure, her inactivity a sign of her own and her husband's status, her idle hours, perhaps, occupied by novel reading. Nancy Armstrong disputes whether in reality middle-class women of the period had either enough time or enough literacy to be the prime novel reading audience.[13] And certainly the majority of 18th-century women novelists wrote out of financial need rather than as a means to fill the long days.

The newness of the form, its low status, its relative easiness to read, offered opportunities for the female author. There was no long and intimidating tradition of 'great masters' and, indeed, some of the forms that contributed to the novel were both accessible and familiar to women – letters, diaries, journals. Virginia Woolf refers to the older forms of literature as 'hardened and set', whereas the novel was open and malleable, 'young enough to be soft in [their] hands'.[14] Moreover, novel writing did not demand a knowledge of the classics, of rhetoric, or of poetic devices – knowledge which was unlikely to be part of female education. George Eliot, lamenting the proliferation of 'silly novels by lady novelists' rather bemoaned the 'absence of rigid requirement' in novel writing; Virginia Woolf, irked that she had never been taught Greek, was probably glad of the fact.[15]

Novel writing, unlike writing for the theatre, is a domestic form of production. Judith Shakespeare, we remember, could not satisfy her theatrical interest by writing plays in Stratford and sending them off by post to the Globe; it was necessary for her to go to London, to be part of the process of production and performance. Michelene Wandor suggests that this has been a continuing problem for women playwrights – and equally, one could add, for women directors. Their visibility, their 'public control of an imaginative world (the action on the stage)' makes them 'a far greater threat than the female novelist to the carefully maintained dominance of men as the custodians of cultural creation'.[16] In patriarchal thinking the public woman, acting outside the confines of proper domesticity, no longer 'the angel in the house', is the whore. Hence Judith Shakespeare's interest in the theatre leads only to seduction and suicide, and generations of mothers have been warned not to put their daughters on the stage. Novels, on the other hand, as the biographies of 18th- and 19th-century female novelists reveal, were written in the drawing-room or in the kitchen or at a dining-room table. The writing, fitted in between domestic tasks, did not have to disturb the equanimity of the household, and the aspiring female novelist demanded no expensive equipment. As Virginia Woolf tells us with about equal amounts of ironic humour and seriousness:

> The cheapness of writing paper is, of course, the reason why women have succeeded as writers before they have succeeded in the other professions.[17]

Domestic production meant also that the woman novelist could maintain a suitable, feminine reticence; in fact, if she wished to use a pseudonym, she could remain anonymous. A husband or father could act as her agent and link with the public world. If she *had* to involve herself in her work's publishing progress it could be by letter rather than through face-to-face contact.

Some of the most suggestive of recent criticism has looked to what is termed the 'feminisation' of culture to account not only for the rise of the woman novelist, but for the growing emphasis in literature on feminine subject matter – the domestic, the interpersonal, feeling – and a feminine point of view – conciliatory, socially minded rather than ego-centred, healing division and difference. Such a perspective was not confined to the female novelists but was present also in the work of their male colleagues, indicating a general anxiety about the most masculinist aspects of the changing society.[18] The contradictions in this feminising process for the woman author are well attested: she gains status as a writer during a period when women are losing political power; she creates, and yet is constrained by, a certain construction of femininity; she finds a public voice and employs it to extol private virtue.[19] In criticism the problem has been that many commentators have not seen the feminisation of culture in a social and ideological context; rather they have viewed it as some natural consequence of the advent of the woman author. The argument roughly goes: women are very involved in the home and small town life, and in a sensitive engagement with social relations; these elements also constitute, in a large measure, the subject matter of novels; hence women are more predisposed to writing novels than to writing in any other genre. In this thesis culture and biology are conflated and, as it is a view that has particularly dogged the analysis of women writers, it is one that I would like to return to in the final section.

I think links can be made between women as novelists and women as short story writers. If we are talking about new forms and low status then the short story is even newer and lower than the novel. Many critics of the short story have stressed that it is not the primary literary form of our period, that it holds a marginal and ambiguous position in literary culture, and that it is peopled with characters who are in some way at odds with the dominant culture. We can look to Frank O'Connor's oft-quoted comment that the short story deals with 'submerged population groups'; Ian Reid claims that the 19th-century French short story tended to be regional rather than metropolitan, portraying characters who were 'aliens'; Declan Kiberd talks of the short story flourishing 'on any cultural frontier'.[20] Although none of these critics actually mention women – an oversight that speaks volumes – we can see in the image they offer of the short story writer and character – non-hegemonic, peripheral, contradictory – a reflection of the position of women in a patriarchal society.

Of course, the short story is also domestically produced and there has been the suggestion that short stories, because of their brevity, are easier for women to write. Virginia Woolf in what seems to me a curious passage, contends that women's fiction would become 'shorter, more concentrated'.[21] This would be prompted by the different 'physical conditions' of women, their inability to enjoy 'long hours of steady and uninterrupted work', and the specific nature of 'the nerves that feed the [female] brain'. All manner of problems are raised by these comments. Woolf seems to believe that shorter forms are somehow easier and need less labour than the longer forms, though one would have thought that her own writing career would have raised doubts in her mind about that. Moreover, considering the aplomb with which Victorian women novelists turned out three-decker novels, why should women now feel uncertain about writing at length? Woolf moves in an unsettling way between a materialist interpretation – she asks the necessary question: how many available writing hours has a woman with children and/or domestic responsibilities – and rank biologism – it's all down to 'nerves'. The phrase 'physical conditions' is so ambiguous that it is unclear whether the reference here is to the material world or to the physiological. Or am I reading this passage too negatively? Perhaps Woolf's appeal for 'an elaborate study of the psychology of women by a woman' points us towards recent studies on the construction of the subject and its relation to literary form and genre. The work that has already been done, in reference to the novel, to modernist forms, or to l'écriture féminine must be only the start of a debate, and certainly the drift of Woolf's argument asks us to take seriously the links between gender, genre and the psychic.

THEORETICAL PROBLEMS

One of the continuing problems and interests for feminist criticism is that the concept of sexual difference can be used to promote both reactionary and radical politics. G. H. Lewes, writing in 1852, structures his thesis on 'lady novelists' around the concept of sexual difference. He writes:

> Of all departments of literature, Fiction is the one to which by nature and by circumstances, women are best adapted. Exceptional women will of course be found competent to the highest success in other departments; but speaking generally, novels are their forte. The domestic experiences which form the bulk of woman's knowledge finds an appropriate form in novels; while the very nature of fiction calls for that predominance of Sentiment which we have already attributed to the feminine mind. Love is the staple of fiction, for it 'forms the story of a woman's life.' The joys and sorrows of affection, the incidents of domestic life, the aspirations and fluctuations of emotional life, assume typical forms in the novel. Hence we may be prepared to find women succeeding better in *finesse* of detail, in pathos and sentiment, while men generally succeed better in the construction of plots and the delineation of character. Such a novel as 'Tom Jones' or 'Vanity Fair', we shall not get from a woman; nor such an effort of imaginative history as 'Ivanhoe' or 'Old Mortality'; but Fielding, Thackeray, and Scott are equally excluded from such perfection in its kind as 'Pride and Prejudice', 'Indiana', or 'Jane Eyre': as an artist, Miss Austen surpasses all the male novelists that ever lived; and for eloquence and depth of feeling, no man approaches George Sand.[22]

Two aspects of this passage are particularly striking. Firstly, Lewes attributes women's involvement in novel writing to both 'nature' and 'circumstance', a combination of historical factors with what he sees as women's innate propensity towards that particular form. The common subject matter of the novel – 'domestic experiences' and 'sentiment' – is to Lewes the 'natural' material for the woman writer; both her social position and her biology lead her in that direction. Secondly, in the allocation of male and female characteristics in writing the preeminent position is given to the male. Women show 'finesse of detail', 'pathos and sentiment', 'eloquence and depth of feeling'; the male writer excells in 'construction of plots', 'delineation of character' and 'imaginative history'. Women thus provide emotion and embellishment; the fundamental construction of novels and the conveyance of wide-ranging and significant meaning remains with the male. A hundred years later Ian Watt in *The Rise of the Novel* followed much the same line.[23] There is the obligatory praise for Jane Austen and her ability 'to reveal the intricacies of personal relationships', and reference to 'feminine sensibility' as if this is a generally understood and unproblematic term. Unlike Lewes, Watt does not explain sexual difference in terms of biology; rather in his reference to J. S. Mill he adopts a position which is liberal, sociological and cultural. But the conclusion of his argument returns to the familiar criticism of women writers and readers who have led the novel into a 'characteristic kind of weakness and unreality' and into 'a certain narrowing of the framework of experience and permitted attitude'. Watt's criticism exemplifies that double-bind which places women's writing in restricted categories and then uses that restriction as a sign of women's creative limitations. A similar pattern of argument has been true of the short story. To say that the woman writer would adopt the short story because of the intimacy of the form, the one-to-one relationship between author and reader, or because of the short story's focus on a manageable, single incident is, on the one hand, to recognise women's social experience in our culture and where that experience may take them in their writing; on the other hand, it is to confine women once again in the personal, the closely detailed, the miniature. By implication the short story becomes both a lesser form and about all that women can manage.

Feminism's response to the reactionary concept of sexual difference is varied. One school embraces the notion of feminine values but, rather than seeing these as inferior to the masculine, valorises the difference and locates in the feminine an important oppositional role. Another group stresses that difference is socially constructed and seeks to interrogate and deconstruct our concepts of masculinity and femininity, exposing their fictive nature. Such perspectives encourage a different approach to women and the short story. Perhaps for some women writers their interest in this form has arisen, not from their belief that it is known and safe, but from their hope that the flexible, open-ended qualities of the short story may offer a transforming potential, an ability to ask the unspoken question, to raise new subject matter. Patricia Stubbs suggests such an interpretation concerning the female short story writers at the turn of the century. Hermione Lee also indicates this possibility in her introduction to *The Secret Self.*[24]

I want finally to look a little more closely at Hermione Lee's introduction because it highlights various problems about attempts to define women's writing. Having subtitled the volume 'Short Stories by Women', Lee inevitably has to ask whether there is something distinctive about the female short story writer, some characteristics common to all or most of them, and not to be found in the work of male short story writers. From the start Lee wisely shows a guarded response to essentialist and prescriptive views. Hence she does not accept that the short story by women is necessarily an expression of emancipatory zeal, nor does she believe that there is a female tradition of writing that is independent of a male tradition, and, of course, she rejects any idea that the female short story can be labelled 'better' than the male.

Lee's hesitancy is understandable, for any attempt to locate the specificity of women's writing is fraught with difficulties. We may find a group of women authors whose writings seem in many ways similar. But then we will discover a much larger group of women authors from the same period and culture whose writings are significantly different from the first, and a group of male writers who seem to be writing rather like the women writers. In short it is never possible to produce the definitive evidence to prove that 'x' is the writing of a woman and 'y' the writing of a man. Most studies that attempt such definitions end by offering qualified suggestions and contending that we need more stylistic analysis to really substantiate any proposition.[25] Furthermore, how can we ever know that the similarities between any group of writers are determined by sex, rather than by race, class, literary form, conditions of literary production, or any combination of any number of factors? Indeed, in finding similarities between groups of writers, could we be employing a self-fulfilling prophecy? Given the complexity of writing, the mass of evidential data it offers, it is hardly surprising that similarities are found. Finally, any attempt to define writing as 'male' or 'female' ignores the ambiguity of writing, its bisexuality, its ability to articulate both masculinity and femininity within the same text.

The problem for Lee is, having rejected attempts to characterise a definitive female writing, what theory of gender and genre can she offer in its place; it is at this point that the analysis becomes unsure. The paragraph that begins with a rejection of 'a separatist aesthetic theory of the 20th-century woman's short story' ends with the comment:

> But it could be said that some distinctive angles of vision and ways of expression are apparent in this selection, which would not be found in an anthology of stories by men.[26]

Lee here seems to be reaffirming the claim that there *is* a specifically female way of writing, that there are both perceptions and stylistic modes that are particular to women. Inevitably this has to be modified. Thus when she refers to women's stories about the tension between the child and the adult worlds she adds – 'This subject is not, of course, a female prerogative. . .'. For Lee the problem of finding a concept of gender that she can relate to the short story proves intractable. Progressively, gender as a critical category disappears from the introduction. We end with 'the secret self'. Is this 'secret self' engendered or is it some ungendered human essence? The queries are all still before us. What is the relationship of gender to writing? Should we talk of the female author or of feminine writing? Does the relationship differ with different literary forms and is there, therefore, a particular scope in relating gender to the short story? Can we create a criticism which is non-essentialist, non-reductive but subtly alive to the links between gender and genre?

Notes

1. Some of the material contained in this paper was considered in a more abbreviated form in my introduction to the relevant chapter in my reader, *Feminist Literary Theory: A Reader* (Oxford: Basil Blackwell, 1986).
2. I do not mean that these forms are written exclusively by male or

female authors, or that an author will have some natural facility for writing in a particular form. It is, of course, noticeable that, with the exception of cultural studies investigations into the Western, James Bond books and such like, there has been even less work on the relationship between the male author and genre, or masculinity and genre. This must link with the reluctance by male critics to problematise masculinity. Gender has become a women's issue. Male writers are simply writers; women writers remain women writers.

3. Jane Spencer, *The Rise of the Woman Novelist: From Aphra Behn to Jane Austen* (Oxford: Basil Blackwell, 1986), p. viii.
4. Virginia Woolf, *A Room of One's Own* (New York: Harcourt Brace Jovanovich, 1963), pp. 69 and 80.
5. Aurora Leigh, *Tablet*, 29 November 1856, p. 762. Quoted in Elizabeth K. Helsinger, Robin Lauterbach Sheets, William Veeder, *The Woman Question: Literary Issues, 1837–1883* (Manchester University Press, 1983), p. 39.
6. Indeed Sandra Gilbert and Susan Gubar in their introduction to *Shakespeare's Sisters: Feminist Essays on Women Poets* (Bloomington & London: Indiana University Press, 1979) argue that it is the lyric with its 'strong and assertive "I"' (p. xxii), that is the real problem for women poets, that in a wider sense the form can be seen as dangerous and challenging. All this confirms that there is much interesting work still to be done.
7. For two contrary views on this question see: Ellen Morgan, 'Human Becoming: Form and Focus in the Neo-Feminist Novel', in Cheryl L. Brown and Karen Olson (eds), *Feminist Criticism: Essays on Theory, Poetry and Prose* (New Jersey and London: The Scarecrow Press Inc., 1978); and Elizabeth Cowie *et al.*, 'Representation vs. Communication', in ed. Feminist Anthology Collective, *No Turning Back: Writings from the Women's Liberation Movement 1975–80* (London: The Women's Press, 1981). Of related interest is Susan Gubar's essay, 'The Birth of the Artist as Heroine: (Re)production, the Künstlerroman Tradition, and the Fiction of Katherine Mansfield', in Carolyn G. Heilbrun and Margaret R. Higonnet (eds), *The Representation of Women in Fiction* (Baltimore and London: The Johns Hopkins University Press, 1983).
8. Dorothy Richardson, *Pilgrimage I* (London: Virago, 1979), p. 9.
9. Ellen Moers, *Literary Women* (London: The Women's Press, 1978), p. 90. See also Rosemary Jackson, *Fantasy: The Literature of Subversion* (London: Methuen, 1981); Eva Figes, *Sex and Subterfuge: Women Writers to 1850* (London: Macmillan, 1982); Jane Spencer, *The Rise of the Woman Novelist: from Aphra Behn to Jane Austen* (Oxford: Blackwell, 1986); Tania Modleski, *Loving with a Vengeance* (London: Methuen, 1984); Joanna Russ, 'Somebody's Trying to Kill Me and I Think It's My Husband: The Modern Gothic', *Journal of Popular Culture*, vol. 6, no. 4.
10. See, for example, Janice A. Radway, 'Women Read the Romance: The Interaction of Text and Context', *Feminist Studies*, vol. 9 (1983) no. 1.
11. Alison Light, '"Returning to Manderley" – Romance Fiction, Female Sexuality and Class', *Feminist Review*, 16 (1984), p. 9.
12. Woolf, *A Room of One's Own*, p. 69.

13. Nancy Armstrong, 'The Rise of Feminine Authority in the Novel', *Novel*, vol. 15, part 2 (Winter 1982), p. 128.
14. Woolf, *A Room of One's Own*, p. 80.
15. George Eliot, 'Silly Novels by Lady Novelists' (1856), in *Essays of George Eliot*, ed. Thomas Pinney (London: Routledge & Kegan Paul, 1963) p. 324.
16. Michelene Wandor, 'The Impact of Feminism on the Theatre', *Feminist Review*, 18 (1984), p. 86.
17. Virginia Woolf, 'Professions for Women', in *The Death of the Moth and Other Essays* (London: Hogarth, 1981).
18. See Terry Eagleton, *The Rape of Clarissa* (Oxford: Basil Blackwell, 1982) and Spencer and Armstrong noted above.
19. Juliet Mitchell, *Women: The Longest Revolution* (London: Virago, 1984) has valuable comments on how in the novel women 'create themselves as a category: women'.
20. Frank O'Connor, *The Lonely Voice* (London: Macmillan, 1963), p. 18; Ian Reid, *The Short Story* (London: Methuen, 1977), p. 24; Declan Kiberd, 'Story Telling: The Gaelic Tradition', in eds Patrick Rafroidi and Terence Brown (eds), *The Irish Short Story* (Gerrards Cross, Buckinghamshire: Colin Smythe Ltd, 1979), p. 20.
21. Woolf, *A Room of One's Own*, p. 81. Reference is also for other quotations in this paragraph.
22. G. H. Lewes, 'The Lady Novelists', *Westminster Review*, vol. 11 (1852) p. 133.
23. Ian Watt, *The Rise of the Novel: Studies in Defoe, Richardson & Fielding* (London: Pelican, 1972) pp. 338–40, from which the following quotations are taken.
24. Patricia Stubbs, *Women and Fiction: Feminism and the Novel, 1880–1920* (London: Methuen, 1979); Hermione Lee, *The Secret Self: Short Stories by Women* (London: Dent, 1985).
25. See, for example, Deborah E. McDowell, 'New Directions for Black Feminist Criticism', *Black American Literature Forum*, 14 (1980); Josephine Donovan, 'Feminist Style Criticism', *Images of Women in Fiction, Feminist Perspectives*, ed. Susan Koppleman Cornillon (Bowling Green, Ohio: Bowling Green University Press, 1972); Annette Kolodny, 'Some Notes on Defining a "Feminist Literary Criticism"', *Critical Inquiry*, vol. 2 (Autumn, 1975) no. 1.
26. Lee, *The Secret Self*, p. IX.

7

Johnny Panic and the Pleasures of Disruption

ROBERT HAMPSON

In *The Pleasures of the Text* Roland Barthes discusses literature in terms of 'a dialectics of desire' between the text and the reader.[1] He draws on this idea to make a distinction between what he calls the 'text of pleasure' and what he calls the 'text of bliss':

> Text of pleasure: the text that contents, fills, grants euphoria; the text that comes from culture and does not break with it, is linked to a *comfortable* practice of reading. Text of bliss: . . . the text that discomforts . . . unsettles the reader's historical, cultural, psychological assumptions . . .[2]

The opening of B. S. Johnson's story 'Everybody knows somebody who is dead', offers an effective gloss on this distinction:

> So you like the title? That's the first thing, they say here, the *Title*.
> *Conflict*, they say, as well. I should engage my reader in a *Conflict*. There is *Resolution* at the end, I see, skipping ahead. Be calm. I have written before. Trust me, not knowing me.[3]

Johnson presents us, in this opening passage, with a model or formula for the short story, but, by presenting us with that model, he also signals that his own story is going to be a very different kind of short story.

The cleavage that Johnson creates between the model and the story he actually produces parallels the distinction that Barthes makes between the 'text of pleasure' and the 'text of bliss'. By drawing our attention to this formula for the short story, Johnson forces us to consider our unconscious expectations. As a result, the story engages us in an exploration of literary conventions as part of the reading process. In the same way, Johnson's direct address to the reader foregrounds the relationship of reader and writer: by asserting a bond of 'trust' as the basis of that relationship, he immediately casts doubt on the security of our trust in him. 'Trust' becomes problematic, it seems to belong to the model short story, the text that grants euphoria, whereas Johnson's story unsettles and discomforts us and makes us self-conscious.

In *Narrative Discourse*, Gérard Genette presents the text as the locus for a complex interaction between writer and reader. Genette begins with the variable 'narrative competence' of the reader which, arising from practice,

> enables him both to decipher more and more quickly the narrative code in general or the code appropriate to a particular genre or a particular work.[4]

Genette demonstrates how the author relies on this narrative competence in the reader – through which the reader follows the story and makes sense of it. (As Umberto Eco[5] puts it, the reader is inscribed within the work's textual strategy.) But Genette also shows how the author can use the reader's narrative competence not only to guide the reader but also to mislead the reader 'offering him false advance mentions, or snares'.[6] Once the reader has acquired the second-degree competence of being able to detect and outmanoeuvre the snare, the author can then offer false snares, things which appear to be snares but are, in fact, genuine advance mentions, and so on.

Alice Munro's story 'How I met my Husband' is a text that 'plays' with its reader in this way: the reader's role is clearly inscribed within its textual strategy in terms of the creation of expectations and the realisation or disappointment of those expectations. Eco has discussed the way in which discursive structures need a textual operator – the 'topic' – to actualise certain semantic possibilities and to deaden others. The title is an obvious 'topic-marker', and 'How I met my Husband' sets up very clear expectations: we anticipate, probably, a romance between a man and a woman, told from the woman's viewpoint and ending in marriage. Munro's story starts with the female narrator's account of herself as a 15-year-old girl, with the landing of an aeroplane, and with the girl's first meeting with the airman. By the end of the first section we have our man and our woman, and the beginning of some kind of relationship between them:

> I wasn't even old enough then to realise how out of the common it is, for a man to say something like that to a woman, or somebody he is treating like a woman. For a man to say a word like *beautiful*.[7]

So far so good: the expectations set up by the title are being comfortably confirmed.

In the fourth section of the story the developing relationship between the girl and the pilot apparently meets an obstacle, when the pilot's fiancée suddenly arrives. In the words of B. S. Johnson's story, we now have 'Conflict': in the rivalry between the girl and the fiancée. But it soon becomes clear that the fiancée is not a serious rival – in fact, the pilot is in flight from her in both senses of the word. Our expectations of a marriage between the girl and the pilot are thus reinforced, and we now settle back comfortably to wait for the 'Resolution'.

By the end of the fifth section the situation has almost resolved itself: the pilot has taken off in his plane to escape from his fiancée; the fiancée has disappeared in pursuit; and the girl is now waiting for the letter that the pilot has promised to send her:

> The mail came every day except Sunday, between one-thirty and two in the afternoon . . . I would get the kitchen all cleaned and then go up to the mailbox and sit in the grass, waiting. I was perfectly happy, waiting . . . I was always smiling when the mailman got there, and continued smiling even after he gave me the mail and I saw today wasn't the day.

When we are three paragraphs from the end, we begin to realise, with the narrator's younger self, that the letter is never going to arrive. And the girl's sense of shock is, if anything, exceeded by our own. In a story called 'How I met my Husband', here we are, less than a page from the end, and the only eligible bachelor we have noticed so far in the story has just been written off.

It is not until the final paragraph that this problem is solved, when the mailman phones up to ask the girl out:

> He asked if I would like to go to Goderich where some well-known movie was on, I forget now what. So I said yes, and I

> went out with him for two years and he asked me to marry him, and we were engaged a year more while I got my things together, and then we did marry.

The expectations created by the title have, technically, been fulfilled, but the reader cannot help feeling cheated by this ending, since another kind of expectation has been disappointed: the expectation that a story called 'How I met my Husband' will devote most of its narrative to the relationship indicated by the title. Instead, the reader feels puzzled by the casualness of attitude taken towards the husband. In contrast to the detailed narration of her relationship with the airman, the narrator cannot even remember the title of the 'well-known movie' to which her husband took her.

We might feel tempted to try and interpret this discrepancy of narrative attention as some kind of value-judgement on these two relationships – or, more sophisticatedly, as a value-judgement on the reader's expectations, but the narrator gets in first. The last sentence of the story blocks any attempt at interpretation:

> He always tells the children the story of how I went after him by sitting by the mail-box every day, and naturally I laugh and let him, because I like for people to think what pleases them and makes them happy.

The narrator's easy acceptance of her husband's interpretation of events – which we know to be a misinterpretation – makes us hesitate about offering our interpretation. This ending exposes interpretation as a fiction-making activity. More than that, it suggests that interpretation has more to do with pleasing the interpreter than with 'truth'. The invitation to interpret in whatever way you wish undermines any claim to value in that interpretation. Not only then is there the 'unsettling' nature of the ending – where the conclusion that the reader has been encouraged to expect does not occur, and the promise of the title is fulfilled in an unexpected way; where the bond of trust between author and reader has been used to lead the reader up the garden path – but also the reader is prevented from avoiding that uneasiness by some interpretative recuperation of the disruption of expectations. 'I like for people to think what pleases them and makes them happy' identifies the end of interpretation as the security and comfort of the interpreter.

Something similar happens in Sylvia Plath's short story 'Johnny Panic and the Bible of Dreams': the narrative strategies create the situation in which the reader is made to feel that any interpretation of the conclusion would be an evasion of experience. In this story, the narrator is a secretary in a psychiatric clinic. Her job is to type texts of the tapes of analytic sessions, but her real work, as she sees it, is to memorise the tapes for her own record, the 'bible of dreams' of the title. She describes herself as 'a dream connoisseur':

> Not a dream-stopper, a dream-explainer, an exploiter of dreams for the crass practical ends of health and happiness, but an unsordid collector of dreams for themselves alone.[8]

Then the narrator gives us a lengthy account of her own dream, her 'dream of dreams' about 'Lake Nightmare, Bog of Madness', the lake into which 'people's minds run at night'. It is both a dream about dreams, and the dream that contains all other dreams. It is also the story's first trap. The reader accepts the narrative's invitations to interpret, but then gradually realises that, in interpreting the story, he / she has also been interpreting the dream, since, at this point, 'story' and 'dream' are identical and inseparable. The reader, in the process of reading, has aligned himself / herself with the dream-analysts. The narrative has carefully established a loaded opposition between 'dream connoisseur' and 'dream-explainers', and the reader is made to feel guilty at this discovery of their unconscious complicity with those who evade the experience by seeking to explain it. The reader suddenly finds himself / herself inside, not outside, the story – and being judged by the story's values.

The reader's guilty recoil from the 'dream-explainers' is encouraged by the subsequent opposition of the narrator and the secretary of the Observation Ward, Miss Milleravage. This, however, is not her real name, but merely an approximation to it:

> She has a funny name I don't ever quite remember correctly, something really odd, like Miss Milleravage. One of those names that seem more like a pun mixing up Milltown and Ravage than anything in the city phone directory.

It is unsettling to be told that the name given to the character is not the character's 'real name' – it is a breach of narrative etiquette –

and, when we are told that the name is 'like a pun', it is difficult to resist responding with further interpretations. The difficult-to-pronounce 'Milleravage' is, most strikingly, a simple amalgam of 'mill' and 'average'. To the various negative connotations of this name is then added the narrator's description of her person, which begins:

> She wears a grey suit over her hard bulk that reminds me vaguely of some kind of uniform.

As with the opposition of 'dream connoisseur' and 'dream-explainers', the reader has no real choice of sides. The reader is forced into an alliance with the narrator – an alliance that is harder to avoid since no other viewpoint is established that can reflect back on her and since the present tense of the narrative allows no temporal distancing either.

The reader is then rushed by a suddenly speeded-up narrative into the final trap and impaled on an interpretive dilemma. The final pages of the story bring together two different codes – the psychiatric and the religious. On the one hand, we are suddenly forced to question the sanity of the narrator with whom the story has encouraged us to align ourselves. On the other hand, the narrator herself presents her experience in a religious language which has developed consistently from the original opposition between 'dream connoisseur' and 'dream-explainers', and which suddenly activates the implications of the word 'Bible' in the title. Even if our view of the narrator has radically changed, this conflict between psychiatric and religious interpretations cannot break out of – or overturn – the oppositions established by the narrator between the mercenary and the visionary, between a 'crass' and 'sordid' social reality and a deeper reality to which the only possible response is panic. The story gives the reader no way out that does not seem to be an evasion of the experience, a denial of the visionary insight. In the end, the narrative-strategy seems to be sado-masochistic: it revels in its painful details and holds the reader close up against them. It points towards two different conceptions of reality, neither of which can be readily accepted by the reader.

By contrast, Munro's stories seem designed to unsettle the reader in a way that points towards a more liberating sense of 'reality'. Consider, for example, the story 'Material'. Like 'How I met my Husband', this is concerned with fiction-making as a self-protective activity. This story focuses on a writer. It begins:

> I don't keep up with Hugo's writing. Sometimes I see his name, in the library, on the cover of some literary journal that I don't open . . . Or I read in the paper or see on a poster . . . an announcement of a panel discussion at the University, with Hugo flown in to discuss the state of the novel today, or the contemporary short story . . . Then I think, will people really go, will people who could be swimming or drinking or going for a walk really take themselves out to the campus to find the room and sit in rows . . . to hear them say that such and such a writer is not worth reading any more, and that some writer must be read.[9]

It turns out that the narrator is Hugo's ex-wife. Her second husband, an engineer, brings her Hugo's new book, a collection of short stories. She turns her attention first to the photograph on the cover:

> He looked . . . very much as I would have thought he would look by now . . . It did not surprise me that he had got fat but not bald, that he had let his hair grow wild and had grown a full, curly beard. Pouches under his eyes, a dragged-down look to his cheeks even when he is laughing. He is laughing, into the camera. His teeth have gone from bad to worse. He hated dentists, said his father died of a heart attack in the dentist's chair. A lie, like so much else, or at least an exaggeration.

This last sentence is the clue to the whole passage. As laughing 'into the camera' reminds us, the narrator is describing a photograph, a representation; and this cover-photo is obviously the self-conscious creation of a particular image. The same can be said of the biographical sketch of the author:

> Hugo Johnson was born and semi-educated in the bush, and in the mining and lumbering towns of Northern Ontario. He has worked as a lumberjack, beer-slinger, counterman, telephone line-man and sawmill foreman, and has been sporadically affiliated with various academic communities.

The narrator translates this for us:

> *He has been sporadically affiliated with various academic communities.* What does that mean? . . . You would think he came out of the bush now and then to fling them scraps of wisdom . . . you would never think he was a practising *academic*. I don't know if he was a lumberjack or a beer-slinger or a counterman, but I do know that he was not a telephone line-man. He had a job painting telephone poles. He quit that job in the middle of the second week because the heat and the climbing made him sick . . . After he quit, Hugo found a job marking Grade Twelve examination papers. Why didn't he put that down? Examination marker. He liked marking examination papers better than he liked climbing telephone poles.

By decoding the photograph and the biography, Munro alerts us from the outset to her interest, in this story, in the making of fictions and the relation between fiction and 'truth'.

The frame-story of 'Material' is concerned with the narrator's reactions to Hugo's new book, but the bulk of the story is a flashback to her early married years with Hugo, when they rented a house in Vancouver and the landlady's daughter, Dotty, lived in the basement. The 'Conflict' in this framed story arises during the narrator's pregnancy:

> There was a water-pump in the basement. It made a steady, thumping noise. The house was on fairly low-lying ground not far from the Fraser River, and during the rainy weather the pump had to work most of the time to keep the basement from being flooded. We had a dark rainy January, as is usual in Vancouver, and this was followed by a dark rainy February.

Hugo cannot sleep and claims that the pump keeps him awake. Then:

> In the middle of the night in the middle of a rainy week I woke up and wondered what had wakened me. It was the silence.
>
> 'Hugo, wake up. The pump's broken. I can't hear the pump.'
>
> 'I am awake.' Hugo said.
>
> 'It's still raining and the pump isn't going. It must be broken.
>
> 'No, it isn't. It's shut off. I shut if off.'

This is the start of a long quarrel between the couple. She wants him to turn the pump back on, and he refuses. Eventually she falls asleep. When she wakes up, Hugo has gone and the pump is thumping 'as usual', but also Dotty is knocking on the door to say that her basement-flat has flooded. The basic theme of 'Material' is how people protect themselves from reality – and an important aspect of that theme is the particular protection that men seem to expect from women. The narrator did not fulfil this role for Hugo – nor did she completely reject it and force Hugo to face reality – and her failure to do one or the other led to the breakdown of the marriage:

> The quarrel between us subsided [but] . . . it was never really resolved . . . I said you don't realize, you never realize, and he said, what do you want me to say? Why do you make such a fuss over this . . . I wondered too. I could have turned on the pump, as I have said, as a patient realistic woman, a really married woman, would have done . . . or I could have told Dotty the truth . . . I could have told somebody, if I thought it was that important, pushed Hugo out into the umpleasant world and let him taste trouble. But I didn't.

Now, in the frame-story, when she sits down to read Hugo's book, she discovers that it contains a story about Dotty. More important, she realises that 'this story of Hugo's is a very good story':

> There is Dotty lifted out of life and held in light, suspended in the marvellous clear jelly that Hugo has spent all his life learning how to make . . . Dolly was a lucky person, people who understand and value this art might say . . . she was lucky to live in that basement for a few months and eventually to have this done to her . . . She has passed into Art. It doesn't happen to everybody.

There are obviously certain critical undertones to this passage and the ironic tone is unmistakable but, nevertheless, at this point, the narrator feels generally appreciative of Hugo's achievement. She had not really believed in Hugo's talent before; now she feels that she should write to him to make up for her earlier doubt. She also sees, for the first time, that her first and second husbands 'are not really so unalike':

> Both of them have managed something. Both of them have decided what to do about everything they run across in the world, what attitude to take, how to ignore or use things . . . They are not *at the mercy*. Or think they are not. I can't blame them, for making whatever arrangements they can make.

With this perception, the various strands of the story seem to be drawing together: Hugo seems to have justified, at last, the 'protection' he demanded by producing the 'words'; the narrator seems to have come to terms with him and resolved their 'quarrel'; Hugo and Gabriel, who have seemed so different and so distinct, have been brought into some kind of relation with each other; and the two sides of the story, the frame- and framed-tale, have been brought together. The reader anticipates a comfortable resolution, but the story does not end here, and it does not end on this note of acceptance.

When the narrator sits down to write the letter of 'acknowledgement' that she has been thinking of sending to Hugo, it takes an unexpected turn, and the terms of her earlier acceptance are echoed and reversed:

> I began to write short jabbing sentences that I had never planned: 'This is not enough, Hugo. You think it is, but it isn't.' I do blame them, I envy and despise.

After the disruptive intrusion of this burst of anger, the story actually ends with Gabriel, and it ends in a way that at last makes clear the connection between the two men:

> Gabriel came into the kitchen before he went to bed, and saw me sitting with a pile of test papers and my marking pencils. He might have meant to talk to me, to ask me to have coffee, or a drink, with him, but he respected my unhappiness as he always does; he respected the pretence that I was not unhappy but preoccupied, burdened with these test papers: he left me alone to get over it.

Hugo is protected from experience by using it as material for his own fictive structures, creating structures that contain and control it. He is protected too by the social role that his fiction-making and his sex give him. Gabriel protects himself from painful experience by ignoring it. The narrator pretends that she is not unhappy – and he pretends not to know that she is. The narrator's letter to Hugo – and the position the narrator has reached by the end of the story – challenge both these techniques of self-protection. At the same time, the narrator's letter is also a challenge to the reader. Not only does it disrupt the mood of acceptance, it also blocks the reader's attempt at fictive closure. In effect, it enacts in relation to the reader the wish expressed earlier in relation to Hugo:

> I would claw his head open to pour my vision into it, my notion of what had to be understood.

And the final words of the story ('he left me alone to get over it') maintain that resistance to closure by the ambiguous balance of 'he left me alone', poised between the anger of emotional neglect and the grateful acceptance of non-interference.

In 'Memorial', Munro again takes self-protection as her theme. She explores the way in which psychological and literary training can operate as a means of evading disruptive experiences by 'explaining' and 'understanding' them. The story works through the contrast of two sisters. Eileen, an English graduate, from whose viewpoint the story is told, is visiting her sister, June, a psychology graduate, for the funeral of June's son. This death is the first potentially-disruptive experience of the story, but June shows no sign of disturbance, no sign of needing help or consolation. She is controlled, efficient and busy making arrangements for a memorial party. Eileen observes:

> Here was a system of digestion which found everything to its purposes. It stuck at nothing. Japanese gardens, pornographic movies, accidental death. All of them accepted, chewed and altered, assimilated, destroyed.[10]

For most of the story, Eileen stands in contrast to this efficient assimilating and protective system: her life 'took shape any way, at all, blown apart by crises, deflected by pleasures'. When she slips away from the memorial party to lie down, her thoughts articulate this opposed position:

> People die; they suffer, they die . . . Illness and accidents. They ought to be respected, not explained. Words are all shameful . . . silence the only possible thing.

Later, when she awakens, she goes for a glass of water and runs into June's husband, Ewart, and her response to him, though unexpected, is in accord with the description we have been given of her:

> Eileen was a hospitable woman, particularly when drunk. This embrace did not exactly take her by surprise . . . And she permitted, she almost welcomed it, how could she extricate herself without gross unkindness? Even if this had not been in her plans, she could shift her expectations around enough to make room for it . . .

This maintains the contrast between Eileen and June: it shows Eileen 'deflected by pleasures'; it suggests a responsiveness to (and respect for) the random and accidental. However, as the narrative proceeds, Eileen's *modus vivendi* becomes more clearly defined, and the contrast between the two sisters is replaced by a parallel:

> What Eileen meant to Ewart, she would tell herself later, was confusion. The opposite of June, wasn't that what she was? . . . The brief restorative dip. Eileen is aimless and irresponsible, she comes out of the same part of the world accidents come from. He lies in her to acknowledge, to yield – but temporarily, safely – to whatever has got his son, whatever cannot be spoken of in his house. So Eileen, with her fruitful background of reading, her nimble habit of analysis (material and direction different from June's, but the habit not so different, after all) can later explain and arrange it for herself.

Before the reader's eyes, the narrative's explanation of the event reveals itself as Eileen's explanation. Eileen's narrative competence is drawn on to 'explain and arrange' for herself the potentially disruptive incidents of her life, just as June draws on her psychological training to 'explain', structure and control the potentially disruptive. The methodology is less obvious, but the effect is the same: the system they have acquired protects them, but it also alienates them. When she was lying on the guest-room bed, Eileen's last thought, before she fell asleep, had been:

> The only thing that we can hope for is that we lapse now and then into reality.

But, by the end of the story, we have seen how any 'lapse' into reality is immediately recuperated by the interpretive systems of the two sisters, and the story ends with a sense of alienation and desolation, as the sisters in their different ways attempt to approach each other emotionally: June offers an account of her son's death (information which has been withheld from the reader up to this point), and Eileen catches a glimpse of her own face in the bedroom mirror 'surprising her with its wonderfully appropriate look of tactfulness and concern'. But behind this image:

> She felt cold and tired, she wanted mostly to get away. It was an effort to put her hand out. Acts done without faith may restore faith. She believed, with whatever energy she could summon at the moment, she had to believe and hope that was true.

At the same time, the reader is aware that Eileen's method of self-protection draws on methods of interpretation that, by ascription, resemble the reader's own. In her interpretation of her encounter with Ewart, Eileen proceeded through character analysis, structural opposition, to symbolic reading. As with 'Johnny Panic and the Bible of Dreams', the reader becomes self-conscious: readers are made aware of their own interpretive activity. Here, however, that awareness is not part of a narrative strategy to trap the reader but rather pushes readers towards a transcendence of their customary methods of interpretation. Instead of forcing on the reader a vision of reality to which panic is the only possible response, Munro edges us towards a sense of reality as something beyond human constructions of it.

It is from this point that the last story I want to consider, 'Walking on Water', takes off. As with 'How I met my Husband', the title of the story creates certain expectations, which the narrative reinforces, but, where the title 'How I met my Husband' creates the straightforward expectation of a male/female relationship with a particular narrative outcome, 'Walking on Water' creates expectations that are beset by a variety of doubts. The angle of vision for the story is provided by Lougheed, a retired chemist who lives in a rooming-house with people much younger than himself, representatives of the counter-culture of the early 1970s. To begin with, we are uncertain whether the title is to be taken literally or figuratively. When we learn that the story involves a young man's promise literally to walk on water, our uncertainty of response to this promise is momentarily put in abeyance by other doubts. First, we have Lougheed's doubt that the story that Eugene has promised to walk on water is some kind of misrepresentation or misunderstanding of the young man. Then, when this doubt has been resolved, the narrative repeatedly plays with the possibility that some kind of 'hoax' or 'joke' is involved. But, despite the rationalisations that these doubts tentatively proffer, the main focus of the narrative falls on the question whether Eugene will succeed in walking on water. This is a very different kind of expectation from that created by 'How I met my Husband': it not only involves uncertainties about the outcome of the story, it involves uncertainties about the genre or sub-genre to which the story belongs, the mode in which it is written (realistic or fabulous), and it also threatens to challenge the reader's conception of reality. In retrospect, 'Walking on water' can also be seen to be an accurate figure for the balancing act that Munro performs in this story.

Munro's narrative strategy in 'Walking on Water' is to proliferate ambiguities and uncertainties. From the outset, the age gap that is built into the narrative's angle of vision acts as a kind of disorientation device. Although Lougheed is represented as retaining more openness of mind than his contemporaries, he is nevertheless brought into contact with a culture which is alien to him. There is, for example, the sign that is painted on his door by the tenants downstairs. When Eugene re-assures him that it is not a magic sign, Lougheed responds:

> I wasn't worried about it being a – sign . . . I was worried about them defacing my door.[11]

And Lougheed is described as being 'dumbfounded by the possibility that such a thing, a sign on a door, could have real meaning for someone who was not a total fool'. Similarly, when Lougheed recalls when he first moved into the house, he remembers 'Miss Musgrave, who was crazy, but in a familiar way', whereas, with the 'present crew':

> it was beyond him, always beyond him, to judge whether they were crazy or not. Even Eugene. Most of all Eugene.

Eugene's explanation of his promise to walk on water expresses clearly the use Munro makes of this generation gap in her story. Eugene tells Lougheed:

> The world that we accept – you know, external reality – . . . is nothing like so fixed as we have been led to believe.

As in 'Johnny Panic and the Bible of Dreams', different ways of seeing, different views of reality, are set against each other; and, as in that story, those different views can be classified as either the rational and the visionary or the rational and the insane; but, while 'Walking on water' maintains a similar ambivalence, it has none of the pain and violence of Plath's story.

The central ambiguity in Munro's story is the status to be accorded to Eugene. In the initial discussion of Eugene's promise, one of the old men observes 'He's either cracked . . . Or else he's Jesus Christ'. The narrative that follows alternately supports alternative interpretations along these lines. On the one hand, we are told about his earlier breakdown; on the other hand, we are informed of his extensive reading in philosophical, religious and occult literature. The ambiguity is present in the description of his characteristic manner:

> Eugene in all the ordinary movements and exchanges of life was an achievement, in the face of something he did not mention. His breakdown? His bursting knowledge? His understanding?

This ambiguity continues in the account of his attempt to walk on water. To the audience watching he clearly fails to walk on water, but Eugene himself emerges from the water sounding 'nearly triumphant'. And how do we evaluate his subsequent speech:

> . . . if this has been disappointing for you it has been very interesting and wonderful for me and I have learned something important.

Is this madness or vision? The end of the story leaves this question open: Eugene just disappears, and we have no way of knowing whether he has merely gone away, or committed suicide, or died in making a second attempt, or in some way succeeded on a second attempt.

The open-endedness of the narrative is played against the open-endedness of a second, intertwined story. Like the narrator of 'Johnny Panic and the Bible of Dreams', Mr Lougheed tells us his dream. This is a recurring dream with a basis in his own past. He tells us, first, the episode from which the dream derives: a young man 'had been taken away from home . . . after a series of fits'; he had 'returned cured', but, then, had killed his father and mother with a shovel. Lougheed's father and brother had joined the hunt for him – Lougheed himself had been left at home. In the dream, however, Lougheed is with his father and brother, but the dream does not contain the contextualising information about the murder that is available to his conscious mind:

> . . . he knew only that he had to find his boots and hurry out with his father and brother. He did not know where he was going, and it would not dawn on him until he had gone along for a while that there was something they were going to find.

And there is a further complication:

> He never dreamed the dream through to the end. Or he never remembered.

At the same time, he has no conscious memory of the outcome of the story either: he cannot remember whether the search-party ever found the young man. This story is obviously related to the main story about Eugene, but the exact nature of the relationship is not clear. Both stories involve two different ways of knowing or two different states of consciousness. Both lack an end. We are tempted also to connect this young man, whose madness breaks out after he has apparently been cured, with Eugene, who has apparently recovered from a breakdown. This temptation is made stronger, later in the main story, when Lougheed is suddenly supplied with an ending to the dream – an ending which seems to supply the answer to Eugene's mysterious disappearance. Lougheed sees himself walking across a bridge and, looking through the gap where a plank is missing, 'he saw a boy's body spread out, face down' in the shallow water of the river. If the reader needs an ending to Eugene's story, they have to make do with this revelation of the end of the parallel story. But the status of this ending is far from clear:

> Earlier in the day, in fact while he was sitting drinking his coffee in that café, something had come to him, a scene which he took to be the ending of his dream. It was a clear and detailed scene effortlessly retrieved from somewhere – either from the dream or from his memory, and he did not see how it could have come from his memory.

The reader who needs an end to the story has to place their trust in a scene whose source cannot be explained rationally. The story thus inscribes two readers: the reader who can accept the open-endedness of the story and, with that, the possibility of alternate accounts of reality, and the reader who requires narrative closure. But even this second reader has to rely on information from a source which cannot be explained rationally. As in 'Johnny Panic and the Bible of Dreams', the reader is trapped by the narrative, but this trap is designed to unsettle rather than to enclose. It forces the reader to accept that reality exceeds rational accounts of it.

Notes

1. Roland Barthes, *The Pleasures of the Text*, trans. Richard Miller (London: Jonathan Cape, 1976) p. 4.
2. Barthes, p. 14.
3. B. S. Johnson, 'Everybody knows somebody who is dead', *Aren't You Rather Young To Be Writing Your Memoirs* (London: Hutchinson, 1973) p. 127.
4. Gérard Genette, *Narrative Discourse*, trans by Jane E. Lewin (Oxford: Basil Blackwell, 1980) p. 77.
5. Umberto Eco, *The Role of the Reader* (Bloomington: Indiana University Press, 1979) p. 10.
6. Genette, p. 77.
7. Alice Munro, 'How I met my Husband', in *Something I've Been Meaning To Tell You* (Harmondsworth: Penguin Books, 1985) p. 55. (All subsequent citations are to the same edition.)
8. Sylvia Plath, 'Johnny Panic and the Bible of Dreams', *Johnny Panic and the Bible of Dreams* (London: Faber and Faber, 1979) pp. 17–18. (Subsequent citations are to the same edition.)
9. Alice Munro, 'Material', in *Something I've Been Meaning To Tell You*, p. 30. (Subsequent citations are to the same edition.)
10. Alice Munro, 'Memorial', in *Something I've Been Meaning To Tell You*, p. 207. (Subseqent citations are to the same edition.)
11. Alice Munro, 'Walking on Water', in *Something I've Been Meaning To Tell You*, p. 77. (Subsequent citations are to the same edition.)

8

High Ground

NICOLA BRADBURY

'High Ground' is the title story of the contemporary Irish writer John McGahern's third collection – he has also written four novels.[1] It is not the leading story of the volume, however: that one (the first) is called 'Parachutes'. These stories, and these titles, fascinate me, because they are at once (as their altitude suggests) aloof, distinct, cool and yet (as the ambiguities of the titles hint) prepared to enter into a relationship, to establish a stance or line between reader and text: prepared by the writer, as I take it, who creates the taste by which he is to be enjoyed, first by designating the space within which this process is to take place.

It is the relationship between the sense of process and that of design in the short story – specifically, here, in these two stories and in the relationship betwen them – that I want to explore.

Perhaps I had better confess at the outset that you may feel this question is compromised by the writer and the works I have chosen. Though I shall not assume that you have read *High Ground* I expect you will recognise its characteristic preoccupations and procedures: the fascination with personal crises of disappointment and loss, particularly within the family, which seem obscurely to point beyond the personal. These belong not only to this collection and to McGahern's work, but familiarly to the Irish short story, which exploits the capacity to move, as in McGahern's work it quietly does, from the personal to the national, and the emotional to the political, if not overtly, then by implication – though it is occasionally explicit, as in the story here called 'Oldfashioned', where the local Sergeant's son is befriended by the English Colonel and his lady. In 'Parachutes' and 'High Ground' the sorrow of the abandoned lover wandering in the dislocation of Dublin streets, trapped between obsessive memories and the importunities of his drunken friends, or the unease of the young man whose choice between personal loyalty and advancement shifts into the public sphere of politics and job: these constitute intimate crises, but are also felt to be symptomatic of an encroaching national confusion of romantic and historic loyalties and political pragmatism: an identity compromised on the one hand by outdated affiliations and on the other by self-abnegation in a dislocated modernity.

The question arises, whether in this context it is possible to sustain my opening claim that the writer creates the taste by which he is to be enjoyed, first by designating the space within which this process is to take place. Is the space in fact a given: the space of Ireland, and of Irish history (a space in time)? Is the writer bound simply to move within this area? The consistency of tone and the interrelationship of stories within the *High Ground* volume, and McGahern's work as a whole, might be judged either to support or to refute this idea. Figures are recalled, and situations developed; a world is constituted, polarised between the cold alienation of Dublin, and the different chill of a lost country (not named, but thought to be McGahern's own Co. Leitrim). Is this a matter of text or context, within the writer's control, or governing his procedures?

I shall return to these questions and to the Irish tradition later, but for the moment I want to focus on that aspect of consistency which might be regarded as thematic or stylistic, or both together, but which we might all agree seems characteristic both of the author and of the chosen form: that is the predominant quality of self-containment in these stories, which challenges us to approach each one individually. It is this independence of stance, together of course with the wry, exact recognition of everything which qualifies it, all the trammels of circumstance, personal, social, historical, literary even, to which Irish writers from Yeats and Joyce onwards have exhibited such an ambivalent exasperation and reverence: this embattled independence is what allows, and even challenges us to take these stories on analytically, and not primarily as subjectively bound descriptions of the conditions of their generation. This is what makes the stories readable to an audience outside those specific conditions, which makes them literary texts.

It is the conjunction of this embattled independence with the short story form that I want to explore. What is it within the work that tells us, formally, what to expect, and hence determines readerly satisfaction and disappointment; and how is this formal strain related to the matter of the text?

Henry James wrote of the novel form that its distinguishing characteristic is elasticity, the capacity to grow more true to its character in proportion as it strains, or tends to burst, with a latent extravagance, its mould.[2] It is not, in other words, a formal property, but a formal propensity, a capacity, which James sees as the thing which makes the novel what it is: its genetic inheritance, if you like. Given this critical coup with the notoriously anarchic novel form, it is remarkable how resistant to definition the short story has proved: how hard it has been to do more than find two main concerns, with plot and atmosphere, each apparently requiring quite different formal properties: the story and the sketch. Why should the short story be harder than the novel to define? Perhaps because James's technique has not been followed: we have expected to find outlines; but we should perhaps look rather for directions, an inherent determination rather than achieved definition. The notion of determination against definition may even indicate what the link is between matter and form, since we could also interpret this in psychological, or indeed in political terms.

The titles of our stories give us a starting point: or perhaps I should say, a direction. The sense of movement develops between their various available meanings, and in the space between the two titles, and between the titles and us. 'High Ground', for instance, could be geographical or moral; we could think of painterly ground, and bas relief; we can not escape an inherent tension between the verticality of 'high' and the horizontal of 'ground'. Both 'High Ground' and 'Parachutes' work in naturalistic and in symbolic ways, and this is characteristic of the stories too: it may indeed prove to be their determining characteristic. From the volume title *High Ground* to the opening 'Parachutes' we are precipitated into movement, a fall; and we are prevented, too, from moving too fast: it is an impeded movement – so that a sense is developed not merely of space but also of time: together with verticality, there is velocity. If the elasticity of the story form stretches between naturalism and symbolism, it could also be held taut by the space/time rhythmic interchange, and the balance of being and knowing, state and process. What I hope to show is how these stories are held by these two possibilities, between being and knowing, and how this is reflected in the text by the prose rhythms (I do not mean just the stylistic traits, though in this short paper I will concentrate on prose style as it is so immediate to our experience as readers) – the rhythms of statement which are caught between rhythms of discovery and rhythms of recovery: one, if you like, proper to the High Ground of Ireland, and the other to the space which the text creates for itself.

The prose rhythms seem to correspond to the title of 'Parachutes' in their arrested development; and the opening interchange, which I shall quote in a moment, also asserts this tendency through its obliquity. Both rhythms and obliquity could be seen as mimetic of emotional distress; but they also function as the necessary and enabling condition of the narrative: thus answering to both the suggestions of 'Parachutes' – the fall and the salvation – and in this the opening movement anticipates the eventual gently ironic twist by which the 'parachutes' which appear in the last pages of the tale are no machines of prevention at all, but organisms of propagation: the drifting seedheads of thistledown, which rise before they fall, and disperse to create new growth, though at the cost of much waste. They look like the skirts of the dancing girl, and they figure the failed affair: brief, extravagant, but not quite wasted, since it gives the germ of this tale. And if we move, as I suggested we might, from the personal to the political, there is another irony in the translation of military equipment to natural forms, and there is salvation implicit in the undetermined but irrepressible fecundity of the Dublin waste ground where the thistles, and the stories, grow.

That political dimension is immanent though never explicit in the imagery from the first.

> 'I want to ask you one very small last favour.'
> 'What is it?'
> 'Will you stay behind for five minutes after I leave?'
> It was the offer of a blindfold, to accept the darkness for a few minutes before it finally fell.[3]

The opening announcement of foreclosure, the determined, simple cadences, the inversion for the reader of ending and beginning, of darkness and light, the powerful, threatening image of the blindfold, are brilliantly compressed and oblique. This obliquity is made to take the formal mimetic stress of emotional expression: into the deadpan, we read anguish. The direct first person is discreetly harnessed by the deictic construction introducing an emotive metaphor: '*It was* the offer of a blindfold. . .' There is a sequence of short, declarative sentences, stripped of most modifiers and qualifiers, which acts like a stylistic tuning fork to our readerly ear, so that elaboration when it comes reaches its full effect: and the effect is both one of recovery, the recreation of the moment, and of discovery, bringing out the acute sensation of loss. Between these the statement is polarised as achievement *and* failure: being and knowing are set at odds, though vitally interdependent: only in this parting is the quality of relationship between them laid open to our view.

> She turned and walked away. I was powerless to follow. She did not once look back. The door swung in the emptiness after she had gone. I saw the barman looking at me strangely but I did not care. The long hand of the clock stood at two minutes to eight. It did not seem to move at all. She was gone, slipping further out of reach with every leaden second, and I was powerless to follow.[4]

The story follows the circular rhythms of recall; as it began with 'one very small last favour', it ends (Miltonically) 'as we set out'; and implicit in this rondo is the disruption of the parting: a disruption which finds its stylistic counterpart in the narrative decorum of the first person mode (that is, a singleness laid open to view). My argument is that McGahern uses these devices of style – and larger motifs: narrative circularity, repetition and the interplay of space and time – all introduced easily without violence to the illusion of naturalism, but with an ulterior purpose: not to displace naturalism, but within its conventions to express, or explore, or simply activate a different level of significance, which is the one we respond to not just as readers but specifically as short story readers. In promoting the distinct interests of process and of design, he instructs us how to read.

This argument not only supports the double force of a style which is both mimetic and self-conscious, engaging and cool, which we might perhaps expect in an unhappy love story, but it also makes critical room for those occurrences in the text which I think might otherwise be hard to explain or justify. The devices I have in mind range from a series of references to books – the pages of a book, another slim volume, a Roman missal – to the kind of literary discussion which quotes Burns and Hazlitt, or the conversational dissection of the words 'comprehension' and 'apprehension' – terms which we can scarcely suppose to be merely accidental or merely plausible in a naturalistic sense.

These literary joggings of the elbow are reminiscent (perhaps again designedly so) of Joyce – not only in *Dubliners* but in *Portrait* and *Ulysses* too – where issues of language and text serve not only for personal characterisation but also to raise the historical matter of Ireland, colonialism, and domination in religious, economic, and even family and sexual politics.

In 'Parachutes' these textual signals crop up intermittently, and not, I think, simply at random: what happens is that the text oscillates between an inner and an outer space and time, and these shifts are marked by the intrusion of the textual prompts. So the opening movement shows the speaker waiting in a bar for his lover to leave, rushing out to look for her, then coming on a group of friends in another bar: and his private world clashes with their social existence; but we feel the awkwardness through this curious signal:

> Paddy Mulvey was reading a book, his eyes constantly flickering from the page to the door, but as soon as he heard my name called his eyes returned fixedly to the page.[5]

The friends are guarding a brown leather suitcase for Halloran: another cache of secrecy, which will eventually be forced open – to reveal women's underwear and a missal – illustrating, as I take it, both the indecorum and the inutility of such inquisitiveness, and so indirectly endorsing the value of mystery. The pages, the suitcase, the slim volume, do not prompt curiosity in the protagonist: they are the signal for recoil to his own secrets:

> I tried to listen but found the arid, mocking words unbearable. Nothing lived. Then I found myself turning towards a worse torture, to all I wanted not to think about.[6]

The inner space and the pocketed time of memory are given a specific narrative location and duration: dinner a few days before Christmas at her sister's home. McGahern's feeling for locality allows a close match of naturalistic specificity and symbolism here. The claustrophobia is insistently detailed:

> The house her sister lived in was a small semi-detached in a new estate: a double gate, a garage, a piece of lawn hemmed in with concrete, a light above the door. The rooms were small, carpeted. A coal fire burned in the tiled fireplace of the front room.[7]

From this fireplace the cosy prospect of a predictable future is disturbing; but the 'vague unease' is finely slanted through a postmortem on the way home. It is not the polite sidestepping nor the open expostulation of conversation that designates the emotional cramp of the design, but the shifts and returns of mood and tense amongst the verbs in this account. The transposition of conflict to the level of syntax is strangely decent, yet unyielding. This is the precise rhythm of history and future, the circumscription of possibility:

> 'What did you think of them?' she'd asked as she took my arm in the road outside.
> 'I thought they were very nice. They went to a great deal of trouble.'
> 'What did you think of the house?'
> 'It's not my kind of house. It's the sort of house that would drive me crackers.'
> 'What sort of house would you like?'
> 'Something bigger than that. Something with a bit more space. An older house. Nearer the city.'
> 'Excuse me,' she said with pointed sarcasm as she withdrew her arm.
>
> I should have said, 'It's a lovely house. Any house with you would be a lovely house,' and caught and kissed her in the wind and rain. And it was true. Any house with her would have been a lovely house. I had been the fool to think that I could stand outside life. I would agree to anything now. I would not even ask for love. If she stayed, love might come in its own time, I reasoned blindly.[8]

And this is where a hiatus, a shift towards the story's present, confronts us – unlike the romantic escapist Yeats' echo of 'the wind and the rain' – with the inexorable consistency of its experience. The sequence may look superficially inconsequential; but at another level, the following casual remark articulates a continuing theme and links the 'then' and 'now' worlds through their concern with what is and what might have been.

> 'Do you realise how rich the English language is, that it should have two words, for instance, such as "comprehension" and "apprehension", so subtly different in shading and yet so subtly

alike? Has anything of that ever occurred to you?'
This was Mulvey now.
'No, I hadn't realised.'

The pluperfect is exactly right: I hadn't realised, but now I have: that is what the story is about.

'Parachutes' moves in two ways: random, like the drifting seedheads, and determined, like the falling aviator; and the relation between the two could be described as suspension, which is the office of the parachute and the condition of the short story. It is at once provocatively self-referential and engagingly inexplicit. A paragraph ostensibly relating the last moments in the bar, for instance, is also an epitome of the whole tale: but it does not claim to be that, and so the effect is not one of closure, but the statement in which recovery and discovery are exactly poised, where the space has been made for what had to be said. Vocal and balletic rhythms here distance and objectify the feeling which informs the last sentence of this extract, at once coolly controlled and extraordinarily passive and impersonal: 'A whole world had been cut from under me.' This blind fall is carefully prepared:

> They started to quarrel. I bought a last round. It was getting close to closing time. Eamonn Kelly had begun an energetic conversation with himself, accompanied by equally vigorous gestures, a dumbshow of removing hat and gloves, handshakes, movements forward and back, a great muttering of some complicated sentence, replacing of hat and gloves. The Mulveys had retreated into stewing silences. I was bewildered as to what I was doing here but was even blinder still about possible alternatives. A whole world had been cut from under me.[9]

'High Ground' is like 'Parachutes' in several ways: the Irish setting; the first person mode; the negotiation of time through memory; the apprehension of an unstatable future against which the story's present is played out. But it is different too. Less urbane (the setting is rural, the speaker a younger man), less literary, less provocative towards the reader, and stronger in its affirmations. It looks more naturalistic, but the effect is a more direct confrontation with conditions of being; less concern with ways of knowing. Whatever perspective we have on 'High Ground' stresses design more heavily than process. In 'Parachutes' prose and narrative rhythms engage our attention; in 'High Ground' it is contours which require our notice: place is foregrounded, and even time has a solid, almost tactile quality: so the busy man 'won't beat around the bush', while the old Master's walls are hung with ancient calendars that have faded into the paper.

A sense of place is economically and even sardonically sketched in a series of small details approaching visual/verbal puns. Here worldly advance is signalled by a sequence of houses built on each others' insurance money in a sort of domestic cannibalism. Not yet engaged in that world, the young protagonist lets his boat drift, sits with his lover in a borrowed Prefect, goes home to help reroof his father's house: he lives amidst drifting and making do, amidst continuities and reciprocity. The arrivist Senator, however, appears in a different relation to the land:

> He had bulldozed the hazel and briar from the hills above the lake, and as I turned to see how close the boat had come to the wall, I could see behind him the white and black of his Friesians grazing between the electric fences on the far side of the reseeded hill.[10]

He sits on the wall and comes 'to the point'. What he offers young Moran is a 'position'. The issue, through another pun, is one of 'principle': the headship of his old school, where his Master would be turned 'out on the road'. Which way to turn? Where to stand?

This is not answered. The conclusion is low-key and determinedly naturalistic, couched in the Master's conversation from the high stool in the bar ('The downward slope from the high stool is longer and steeper than from the top of Everest.'), where he speaks of high things. He extols the high values of home, of staying still, 'practically at the source of the Shannon'. He claims, 'There are people in this part of the country digging ditches who could have been engineers or doctors or judges or philosophers had they been given the opportunity.'[11] But we hear him through the listener outside, and this perspective complicates the security of place, and suggests the non-naturalistic significance of the moment too. The tale is rounded to a close which holds all the possibilities – the ways of advance, retreat and of evasion – in careful balance: process is captured in design, and the mutual compromise of knowing and being are presented through the narrative contentions of youth and age, and the dimensions of time and space. Perhaps it is worth noting that while 'Parachutes', the disappointed love story which opens the collection, is followed by 'A Ballad', 'High Ground' comes near the middle of the volume, and is held between 'Crossing the Line' and 'Gold Watch'. Between space and time.

In approaching these tales as examples of the short story form I have tried to work within the confines of the individual text and then the collection, taking the line any reader might follow, and exploring how the author has laid down directions, and created both parameters and volume, made the space of the story: in this process, the dimensions of space and time are material for his art. But they are also, of course, the conditions within which he works: there is a context for these texts, both geographical and historical, in literature and in life, and this certainly also conditions our reading and must be taken into account as we look for what I began by calling the 'inherent determination' of the form.

John McGahern, who lives near the border, is writing out of contemporary Ireland, out of an embattled, impoverished and fiercely self-conscious land: one with a peculiar sensitivity to geography and to history. He is also writing out of an Irish tradition, a specific short story tradition, working within these conditions, which provide not only obsessive themes, but also an attitude, a literary tone, poised between dispassionate control and deep engagement. The name I am sure you have been waiting for me to acknowledge is Joyce, and *Dubliners*, like Dublin, is certainly a presence in McGahern's world: not simply (if it can be called simple) through the sense of place, but also through the techniques of oblique progression through a sequence of tales at once separate and interlinked, and through the exposed solipsism of stream-of-consciousness poised against direct speech. But there is also another precursor, whom McGahern himself acknowledges. This is George Moore. His collection of stories, *The Untilled Field*,[12] has a relationship to McGahern's country stories which balances *Dubliners* and the city; both, of course, are subsumed in a larger category of Irish stories, for in both the presence of the other Ireland is felt beneath the surface. Moore, like Joyce, and later McGahern, writes of an Ireland bound in by bigotry and poverty, but also by beauty and pride; an Ireland which cannot be borne but can never wholly be left behind, even though the young emigrés, the 'wild geese', have flocked since the famine to America, while Irish intellectuals have turned to Europe, and particularly to Paris, for a freedom compromised at home by the hold of the church and the irreconcilable demands of political confusion. What Moore calls the 'depopulation question' lies behind every coming-of-age, every romance, every new job or old home, every struggle and betrayal: life is lived, or endured, in the knowledge of a possible exile, possible renunciation, or betrayal, which is both personal and national. George Moore's fine story 'The Wild Goose' ends with a paragraph which *High Ground* could accommodate with ease:

> He left early next morning before she was awake in order to save her the pain of farewells, and all that day in Dublin he walked about, possessed by the great joyful yearning of the wild goose when it rises one bright morning from the warm marshes, scenting the harsh north through leagues of air, and goes away on steady wing-beats. But he did not feel he was a free soul until the outlines of Howth began to melt into the grey drift of evening. There was a little mist on the water, and he stood watching the waves tossing in the mist thinking that it were well that he had left home – if he had stayed he would have come to accept all the base moral coinage in circulation; and he stood watching the green waves tossing in the mist, at one moment ashamed of what he had done, at the next overjoyed that he had done it.[13]

It is not just the emotional and moral territory that we recognise here, but, as I should like to argue, the way we come to know them: the directions implicit in the phrasing itself: the prose rhythms, the balance of literal and figurative language, the nervous accuracy of tense, mood and voice in the verbs, which tell us where the boundaries lie that this tale strains against, and urges the need to overstep. May I give the last sentence again, with this in mind, as a fitting conclusion?

> There was a little mist on the water, and he stood watching the waves tossing in the mist thinking that it were well that he had left home – if he had stayed he would have come to accept all the base moral coinage in circulation; and he stood watching the green waves tossing in the mist, at one moment ashamed of what he had done, at the next overjoyed that he had done it.

Notes

1. John McGahern's works are published by Faber and Faber. They are: *The Barracks* (1963), *The Dark* (1965), *Nightlines* (1970), *The Leavetaking* (1974), *Getting Through* (1978), *The Pornographer* (1979), *High Ground* (1985). Citations from *High Ground* are from this edition.
2. Henry James, *The Art of the Novel: Critical Prefaces*, with an introduction by R. P. Blackmur (New York: Scribner's, 1934, rpt. 1962) pp. 45–6.
3. 'Parachutes', in *High Ground*, p. 11.
4. Ibid.
5. Ibid., p. 12.
6. Ibid., p. 13.
7. Ibid.
8. Ibid., p. 14.
9. Ibid., pp. 15–16.
10. 'High Ground', p. 95.
11. Ibid., p. 102.
12. George Moore, *The Untilled Field* (London: T. Fisher and Unwin, 1903).
13. Ibid., 'The Wild Goose', p. 393.

9

Hemingway and Fitzgerald: Two Short Stories

LIONEL KELLY

As a title 'Hills Like White Elephants' is provocative: what is the meaning of this simile, and what is its relation to the subject of the story? At the same time, the title makes a simple figurative proposition, that one set of things are like another set of things: hills: white elephants. In the event what we learn is that this simile is used by the woman in the story – she is called Jig – both as a response to an observed image, the line of hills in the far distance, and also as a sign to the man; a signal that she is still capable of inhabiting his world, on his terms. So that in the story itself, the sentence from which the title comes is an act of verbal complicity; it is an endeavour of sharing, a desire to see the world in his terms, to say 'bright things', to try new experiences with him, and take things on and therefore to be free with him, unencumbered in the world. The sense of strain, of trying, of endeavour on Jig's part becomes more explicit as we read on: as though the only way to hold on to what they have, or had, is to see things in his terms. This role is becoming less and less tenable for her. At one point, the man proposes: 'We can have everything', and 'We can have the whole world'. These affirmations are opposed to her expression that ' . . . every day we make it more impossible'. Hemingway's presentation of these two and their conversation is very assured. We are given this nervous, edgy, brittle discourse, bordering on anger. The man seeks to reassure Jig, and he resents what he hears as her sardonic tone when she implicitly mocks him:

> 'They look like white elephants,' she said.
> 'I've never seen one.' The man drank his beer.
> 'No, you wouldn't have.'

> 'I might have,' the man said. 'Just because you say I wouldn't have doesn't prove anything.'[1]

The subject here is 'knowledge', which is so often Hemingway's subject. And here, we have a verbal cat and mouse game in which the status of one's knowledge is disputed or mocked: at this moment, knowledge of white elephants, but of course, more seriously, knowledge of the real subject of their conversation, abortion, a topic which is not specified, but expressed through implication. And so, from the advantage of his knowledge, he seeks to reassure her about the operation he is taking her to have; he claims a knowledge of its essentially simple nature:

> 'It's really an awfully simple operation, Jig,' the man said. 'It's not really an operation at all.'
> The girl looked at the ground the table legs rested on.
> 'I know you wouldn't mind it, Jig. It's really not anything.'
> 'It's just to let the air in.'
> The girl did not say anything.

This conversation is set against a briefly, yet tellingly presented physical location; metaphorically, it is a place of stasis; literally, the bar of a railway station in an unnamed town in the Ebro Valley, waiting for the express train from Barcelona to Madrid. The woman Jig appears to be 'innocent' of certain matters, or, to put it another way, without knowledge: of Spanish, for example. She asks the man about what is painted on the bead curtain of the open door of the bar:

> 'Anis del Toro. It's a drink.'
> 'Could we try it?'

They have an Anis each, to which Jig responds: 'It tastes like licorice', and he replies: 'That's the way with everything.' 'Yes,' said the girl. 'Everything tastes of licorice. Especially all the things you've waited so long for, like absinthe.' Here, knowledge derives from experience: anis and water, it turns out, tastes like licorice, as does absinthe; experience that is, tastes the same: the world of possibilities is shrinking; and further, the possible world is shrinking – the abortion. Remember what the man says: 'We can have the whole world', 'We can have everything'; but not the world of childbirth, motherhood, fatherhood. I am being too literal, of course. The man goes on to propose an idea which runs counter to his notions of knowledge; of course, he does this strategically, as a ploy in this verbal conflict; but it is a false note which we hear. And the idea is that in some cases knowledge will not change you, nor will experience: and so he proposes that after the operation, 'We'll be fine . . . Just like we were before'. And, 'That's the only thing that bothers us. It's the only thing that's made us unhappy.' Jig bears and recognises the falseness of this: and we are led into that discussion of a world of possibilities, which she is now increasingly determined to deny, and to insist on, rhetorically, an *a priori* knowledge: 'I don't feel any way,' the girl said. 'I just know things.' From this point on, his efforts to mollify her become increasingly irritating to her, and lead into her famous repudiation of him:

> 'Would you please please please please please please please stop talking!'

We are witness then to this querulous conversation, which proceeds by indirection and understatement, and avoids the specific: he attempts to defuse the emotional drama of the operation: she resists his simplistic reductions. The ultimate point is reached when she resists him by threat:

> 'But I don't want you to,' he said. 'I don't care anything about it.'
> 'I'll scream' the girl said.

And the word 'scream' lies on the page to be counterpointed a little later on on the same page by the word 'reasonably' in this passage: 'He drank an Anis at the bar and looked at the people. They were all waiting reasonably for the train.' The word calls attention to itself: its inappropriateness, as applied to the waiting travellers, is marked: it refers back, of course, to 'I'll scream.'

This is a very short short story, subtly contrived, convincingly worked: it can be used to ask questions about what is central, indeed, what is crucial in our reading of short stories – treatment, or subject. Here, subject, if abortion is the subject, is stated through understatement, through the unspecific: and indeed, to say that the subject is abortion is to risk a crude response. Here, treatment seems to be everything. Notice, for example, the attention to specific physical detail at certain moments, as in this:

> 'The girl looked at the bead curtain, put her hand out and took hold of two of the strings of beads.'
> 'And you think then we'll be all right and be happy.'

Her response to him is conditioned by this physical gesture, which of itself means nothing, but deflects her look away from him, and in so doing, concentrates her reply into a statement of authoritative doubt. And there is the earlier moment which I have already quoted, when we are told how 'The girl looked at the ground the table legs rested on', where the sense of the ground's durable solidity, for resting things on, is opposed to the man's account of what the operation does, how it works: 'It's just to let the air in', a statement, of course, of quite extraordinary brutality. For the duration of the story the girl Jig is the one who seems open to imaginative possibility, based on concrete particulars – the distant hills, the bead curtain, the ground the table legs stand on – and the man is the one of reduced imagination and vision – literally, he cannot see the train coming down the tracks. And yet, it is his world to which the imaginative appeals are made:

> ' . . . But if I do it, then it will be nice again if I say things are like white elephants, and you'll like it?'

Now in this story the narrator shares Jig's imaginative style: and we might be able to infer from this where Hemingway stands in relation to his material here. The story is composed largely of dialogue, but there are some paragraphs of description; this is one:

> The woman brought two glasses of beer and two felt pads. She put the felt pads and the beer glasses on the table and looked at the man and the girl. The girl was looking off at the line of hills. They were white in the sun and the country was brown and dry.

We notice the felt pads here – a calling attention to physical detail which is like Jig's fingering of the beads, and we notice the contrast between the line of hills – white in the sun – and the country which is brown and dry, so that the narrator's view leads into Jig's simile – 'They look like white elephants.' We have thus a proximity between Jig and the narrator, and this is in contrast to our experience of the facile rhetoric of the man's arguments: the only word that might suggest some bond between him and the narrator is that word 'reasonable', and how we respond to that depends on whether we feel it is the man's word, or the narrator's.

I raise this question about where Hemingway is in relation to the material of this story both because of its intrinsic interest, and also because of the title of the volume in which 'Hills Like White Elephants' appeared – *Men Without Women*: and, in addition, having regard to that animus against women which exists in some of his writing, in the novels and the short stories. It may be that one of the features which distinguishes this little story, and contributes to its quality, follows from the treatment which renders Jig's position with poignant sympathy. If we think of the role of some of the women in Hemingway's fiction, it is difficult to resist the view that he thought 'the female of the species to be more deadly than the male'.[2] I have in mind such obvious cases as Helen in 'The Snows of Kilimanjaro'; the wife Margaret in 'The Short Happy Life of Francis Macomber'; Lady Brett Ashley in *The Sun Also Rises*, and the girls, lovers and mothers in his first collection *In Our Time*. No doubt others could be added to this list. 'Hills Like White Elephants' was first published in the magazine *transition* (v) in August 1927, and went into *Men Without Women* which appeared in October of that year. As a title *Men Without Women* has an aggressive ring, appropriating for its concerns exclusively male worlds: the cover decoration of the current paperback edition (Granada) shows a boxer, a soldier and a gangster, who pose for us in a watchfully combatant style. It is difficult to resist the view that we are meant to approve of men who are without women, although the content of some of the stories in the collection qualifies that impression. Hemingway wrote to Scott Fitzgerald about his choice of this title, and the letter is interesting:

> What do you think of Men Without Women as a title! I could get no title, Fitz, run through Ecclesiastics [sic] though I did. . . . Well, Fitz, I looked all through that bible, it was in very fine print and stumbling on that great book Ecclesiastics, read it aloud to all who would listen. Soon I was alone and began cursing the bloody bible because there were no titles in it – although I found the source of practically every good title you

> ever heard of. But the boys, principally Kipling, had been there before me and swiped all the good ones so I called the book Men Without Women hoping it would have a large sale among the fairies and old Vassar Girls.[3]

The tone of this letter is characteristic of the serio-comic style of the correspondence between Hemingway and Fitzgerald at that time, though the remark about Kipling was probably intended seriously. In one of his replies, Fitzgerald refers to a portmanteau modern novel called 'All The Sad Young Men Without Women In Love', but his principal response to *Men Without Women* was very generous: he wrote:

> In spite of all its geographical and emotional rambling, it's a unit, as much as Conrad's books of Contes were. Zelda read it with fascination, liking it better than anything you've written. Her favourite was 'Hills Like White Elephants', mine, barring 'The Killers' was 'Now I Lay Me.'[4]

Fitzgerald went on to quote the opening sentence of 'In Another Country' and added: 'God, what a beautiful line. And the waking dreams in "Now I Lay Me" and the whole mood of "Hills Like" '. I am struck by the fact that Zelda liked 'Hills' most of all – and that Fitzgerald too responded to its mood. I am less convinced than he was of the sense of the collection as a unit, however, and this derives in some measure from the title, which is something of a misnomer. Only four of the stories deal with men who are without women because they are in a theatre of combat: 'Undefeated' and 'Banal Story' about the bullfighter Manuel Garcia; and 'In Another Country', and 'Now I Lay Me' about the war wounded, and Nick Adams before a military offensive. Women feature in many of the other stories, and not always disadvantageously. We might regard 'A Canary for One' as a kind of companion piece to 'Hills Like White Elephants', since it deals with marital despair, and describes a conversation on a train as a husband and wife travel back to Paris to start separate lives. It is not a very good story, in my view, depending for its point on a rather laboured irony, and quite lacks the subtlety of 'Hills'. Perhaps I am wrong to make too much of the title *Men Without Women*: yet, Hemingway's titles are usually very striking, and he worked hard to get them: some of them have a phrasal elegance and resonance which is very arresting, and have a propositional quality in which they stand in oblique unexplained relationship to the subject of the story, such as 'In Another Country', 'Now I Lay Me', 'A Way You'll Never Be', 'A Clean, Well-Lighted Place': and this is where I would place 'Hills Like White Elephants', a fine subtle story in which the title earns its keep as an indicator of an imaginative desire now strained to breaking point.

Fitzgerald was similarly preoccupied with the naming of his books. And the title of his story 'The Lees of Happiness' is properly ambivalent. It first appeared in the *Chicago Tribune* in September 1920, and then went into *Tales of the Jazz Age* of 1922. It has not had a good press from Fitzgerald's critics, though it persistently appears in English collections of his stories. In his critical portrait of Fitzgerald, Henry Dan Piper argues that *Tales of the Jazz Age* illustrates a deterioration in his writing because of the way some of the stories 'naively glamorize' his world, and only excepts 'May Day', 'The Jelly-Bean', and 'The Diamond as Big as the Ritz.' André Le Vot in his more recent biography makes no mention of the story, and in the collection of essays devoted entirely to Fitzgerald's short stories, edited by Jackson R. Bryer,[5] 'The Lees of Happiness' receives two brief comments. One writer sees it as 'another story that works out the sad fate of life in the suburbs – that is, life where the city leaves off and domestic life begins' – a curious reading I think: and another mentions it in relation to Fitzgerald's use of mental illness as a way of explaining a character's inability to function: this too seems to me irrelevant. My own interest in it is of long standing, though I have usually avoided discussion of it, because I formed a sentimental attachment to it which has something to do with its capacity to deal in romantic illusion. Ftizgerald thought well of it. He describes it briefly in a letter to his agent Harold Ober on 17 July 1920 as 'an excellent if somewhat somber story',[6] and a little earlier he had written to his publisher Maxwell Perkins that he had 'Just finished the best story I've done yet . . .'.[7] 'The Lees of Happiness' tells the story of a young writer, Jeffrey Curtain, whose early work has won popular acclaim: he meets and quickly marries Roxanne Millbank, a chorus girl of great beauty, herself on the verge of a glittering career in the theatre: they retire to the country to celebrate their love: within two years he suffers a blood clot on the brain, is totally paralysed, and lives a vegetable existence until his death 11 years later: during this time Roxanne surrenders her life to care of him.

Now I have said that the title is ambivalent: its ambivalence derives from the word 'lees' of course, which means the sediment of a liquid, the basest part, the dregs, the refuse: the O.E.D. cites reference to *Macbeth,* when Macbeth feigns hearing of Duncan's death:

> Had I but died an hour before this chance,
> I had liv'd a blessed time; for, from this instant,
> There's nothing serious in mortality –
> All is but toys; renown and grace is dead;
> The wine of life is drawn, and the mere lees
> Is left this vault to brag of.[8]

Clearly, Jeffrey Curtain's vegetable condition represents, at one level, what the 'lees' of the title implies: the dregs of what was something other: at one point he is visited by a celebrated nerve specialist, who asserts to Roxanne the futility of her care, and when she protests her love, retorts: 'But you can't love that'[9]: the clinical accuracy of the depersonalised 'that' is very telling, and chilling. The specialist leaves, acknowledging her remarkable quality of endurance, and pitying the waste of her life, so that 'lees' now applies to her too. She retains a capacity for love in generalised ways, 'for life, for the people in the world, from the tramp to whom she gave food she could ill afford, to the butcher who sold her a cheap cut of steak across the meaty board. The other phase was sealed up somewhere in that expressionless mummy who lay with his face turned ever toward the light as mechanically as a compass needle and waited dumbly for the last wave to wash over his heart.' Fitzgerald could hardly have called his story 'The Dregs of Happiness', and there is a bonus in the use of this almost archaic word, with its poetic resonance: for 'lees' is also the plural of 'lee', and the primary meaning of 'lee' is shelter, warmth, protection, deriving from the nautical meaning of the sheltered side of an object, and hence, therefore the side away from the wind: thus, as the dictionary puts it, calmness, peace, tranquillity. Fitzgerald was consciously playing on the association between 'lee' and 'lees'. On her marriage to Jeffrey, Roxanne 'retires' from the stage, and after a year of nationwide travel they withdraw from the public world, buy 'an old house and twenty acres near the town of Marlowe, half an hour from Chicago'; and we have the sense that this gilded pair of lovers have chosen a place of deliberate retreat, a haven of pastoral bliss as a backdrop to their intense love. They are visited by Harry Cromwell, who lives in Chicago, and whose story is infolded with theirs. He has made an unhappy marriage, and comes to stay with them whilst his wife Kitty takes their young child to her mother in New York, to recuperate from childbirth. Harry is witness to the isolating passion of Jeffrey and Roxanne, so different from his own experience with Kitty: and the language of pastoral idyll enters into the description of his stay with them:

> Harry's week passed. They drove about the dreaming lanes or idled in cheerful inanity upon lake or lawn. In the evening Roxanne, sitting inside, played to them while the ashes whitened on the glowing ends of their cigars.

When Harry leaves them they are thrilled to be 'alone' again, to have the world reduced to the centrality of their own unity – an ironic prolepsis of that utter estrangement from the world Jeffrey is soon to suffer: a habitation Roxanne voluntarily maintains in her care of him.

Harry Cromwell is presented as a good husband, patient and forbearing; he is a faithful friend, and becomes a sympathetic listener and adviser to Roxanne during the years in which she has to manage on diminishing financial resources: he too is associated with that word 'lees', both because the years of his married life are conditioned by storm and tempest, and because what is left to him is the dregs of that life: of him, as of Roxanne, we are finally told:

> To these two life had come quickly and gone, leaving not bitterness, but pity; not disillusion, but only pain.

He loses his wife to an older richer man, and his child goes with her: he is left with the emotional detritus, the pain of separation, particularly from his child, for which there is no recompense: it is an echo, or a parallel, in properly differentiated terms, to Roxanne's tragic abandonment.

There is a particular incident in the story to which the word 'lees' applies. When Harry first visits them Roxanne is learning how to make biscuits. Her first efforts are a failure, and she comically laments to Jeffrey 'Oh, I'm useless'. 'Turn me out,

Jeffrey – I'm a parasite; I'm no good', another ironic prolepsis of helplessness. However, they seize on Harry's suggestion that the inedible biscuits are decorative, and Jeffrey hammers them into a wall in a perpendicular row 'twelve of them, like a collection of primitive spear-heads'. It is a brilliant stroke, this business of the biscuits, anticipating the surety of Fitzgerald's touch in, for example, the gaudy array of Gatsby's shirts, or the dinner party at the Villa Diana in *Tender Is The Night*. Later, Harry eats these biscuits unthinkingly, hardly aware of what he is doing, and whether he ate the nail with the first one, as he sits alone downstairs, wrapped in the despair of his own marital failure, whilst the specialist is upstairs with Roxanne and Jeffrey. And there is a long paragraph describing the cause of his hunger, which fits both with the representation of his careless sluttish wife, and the consumation of these totem-like objects, which ceremoniously memorialise his first visit to Jeffrey and Roxanne in their pastoral retreat. What we notice is that the eating of these biscuits is a kind of rubicon: the dregs of failure are here turned into nourishment: and at that moment, Roxanne's gilded life turns from one of celebrant passion – in which the sexual element is gently insinuated – to one of ironically pastoral care. It is a brilliant stroke, one which justifies Fitzgerald's faith in the story.

I am not going to claim that 'The Lees of Happiness' is without fault. There is something factitious about the use of a paralysing illness as the *donnée* of a story, though when we think of *Tender Is The Night*, we shan't be too insistent on that. And the handling of Jeffrey Curtain's illness is deftly economic, the brevity of its presentation matching the abruptness of its onset. The bulk of the story deals with the long duration of Roxanne's care of her husband, and the paralleled collapse of Harry's marriage, shifting our attention away from the drama of the illness, disturbing our sense of what the subject of the story is.

Some aspects of Fitzgerald's style here are not entirely secure. In the opening section particularly, but elsewhere too, he goes in for qualifying epithets to excess, as in this paragraph:

> For a year they lived in hotels, travelled to California, to Alaska, to Florida, to Mexico, loved and quarrelled *gently*, and *gloried* in the *golden* triflings of his wit with her beauty – they were young and *gravely* passionate; they demanded everything and then yielded everything again in *ecstasies* of unselfishness and pride.

> She loved the swift tones of his voice and his frantic, unfounded jealousy. He loved her *dark* radiance, the white irises of her eyes, the warm *lustrous* enthusiasm of her smile. [My italics]

Inevitably Roxanne's white dress has a 'frail gorgeousness' about it. This way of writing is indigenous to Fitzgerald's style, of course, and in 'Diamond as Big As The Ritz', in *The Great Gatsby* and elsewhere, it is used symptomatically as one of the means of his critique. Here, the effect is that of over-writing, even if this is not persistently so. On the other hand there is an adroit use of the contrast between surface and depth which leads to a telling image of Roxanne's experience of the immediate aftermath of Jeffrey's illness, presenting the feel of obliquity of vision in which her sense of the centre of things has curiously shifted:

> There is a sort of waking nightmare that sets in sometimes when one has missed a sleep or two, a feeling that comes with extreme fatigue and a new sun, that the quality of the life around has changed. It is a fully articulate conviction that somehow the existence one is then leading is a branch shoot of life and is related to life only as a moving picture or a mirror – that the people, and streets, and houses are only projections from a very dim and chaotic past.

Earlier, we are told, in the deliberately anecodatal opening, that Jeffrey Curtain's work was merely amusing, superficial, glib: it contained 'no deep interior laughs, no sense of futility, or hint of tragedy', phrases which anticipate the events to come, but also suggest Fitzgerald's capacity for a Beckettian sense of tragi-comic absurdity. And the contrast between Roxanne and Harry's wife Kitty is similarly worked in images of surface and depth. Kitty's response to a visit from Roxanne is described thus.

> Her cordiality was strident and intimate, hostility melted so quickly to hospitality that it seemed they were both merely in the face and voice – never touching nor touched by the deep core of egotism beneath.

Kitt's 'deep core of egotism' is displayed rather in the slovenly condition of their apartment, the unwashed child and the effusive vulgar pink of her soiled clothes. These figurative means of differentiation and contrast are artfully used by Fitzgerald, and give real substance to his portrayals.

In a letter to his agent Harold Ober, written in the summer of his collapse in 1935, Fitzgerald wrote:

> . . . all my stories are conceived like novels, require a special emotion, a special experience – so that my readers, if such there be, know that each time it'll be something new, not in form but in substance.[10]

What, we might ask, is the 'special emotion' of this story? Indeed, what is its subject? I find these questions difficult to answer. It appears to be a story about loss, about the collapse of romantic illusions, about failures to achieve the graspable contentments of ordinary life. And yet, equally, it is not about these things at all, but rather about sustenance, the sustaining power of the affections, and the capacity for endurance. These, we may feel, are the 'special emotions' which this sombre story celebrates.

Notes

1. Ernest Hemingway, *Men Without Women* (London: Granada, 1982) p. 44. Subsequent citations to 'Hills Like White Elephants' are to the same edition.
2. Jeffrey Meyers, *Hemingway: A Biography* (London: Macmillan, 1985) p. 110.
3. Carlos Baker, ed., *Ernest Hemingway: Selected Letters 1917–1961* (London: Granada, 1981) p. 260.
4. Andrew Turnbull, ed., *The Letters of F. Scott Fitzgerald* (London: The Bodley Head, 1963) p. 301.
5. Jackson R. Bryer, ed., *The Short Stories of F. Scott Fitzgerald: New Approaches in Criticism* (Wisconsin University Press, 1982) pp. 9 and 49.
6. Matthew J. Bruccoli, ed., *As Ever, Scott Fitz- : Letters Between F. Scott Fitzgerald and His Literary Agent Harold Ober, 1919–1940* (London: Woburn Press, 1973) p. 16.
7. John Kuehl and Jackson R. Bryer, eds. *Dear Scott/Dear Max: The Fitzgerald-Perkins Correspondence*, (New York: Scribners, 1971) p. 31.
8. Peter Alexander, ed., *William Shakespeare: The Complete Works* (London: Collins, 1966) p. 1008. (*Macbeth* Act. 2 Sc. 3, 1.89–94.)
9. F. Scott Fitzgerald, 'The Lees of Happiness' in *The Diamond As Big As The Ritz And Other Stories* (Harmondsworth: Penguin, 1962) p. 233. Subsequent citations to 'The Lees of Happiness' are to the same edition.
10. Op. cit., Matthew J. Bruccoli, *As Ever, Scott Fitz-*, p. 221.

10

Genre Reversals in Doris Lessing: Stories Like Novels and Novels Like Stories[1]

CLAIRE SPRAGUE

Doris Lessing is not unusual in having begun her career with short stories. She is unusual in having continued to write short stories for a long time after she established her reputation as a novelist. In fact, it comes as a surprise to realise that she has stopped writing short stories (at least for now?). Her last volume of new short stories appeared in 1972. (Later volumes have collected previously published short stories.) Nonetheless, her short story writing paralleled her novel writing, perhaps her very best novel writing, for a very long time. Sometimes they preceded and deeply affected her novel writing.

It could be said that Lessing's genius is for the short story, not the novel. *The Golden Notebook* can, like *Middlemarch*, be called 'a bundle of stories loosely tied together'.[2] Its principle of organisation is collage or pastiche, to use the negative word Anna adopts for it in the novel.

There is a special interrelationship between *A Man and Two Women* (1963) and *The Golden Notebook* (1962).[3] The risks of looking back to say this are obvious; hindsight tends to fill in rifts, ignore accidents and smooth rough places. Still, the relationship between these two works, too rich and too provocative to ignore, raises questions that destabilise genre. What is the short story? Is it pastiche (Anna Wulf's word) or montage (my word)? Such questions join other unsettling questions in *The Golden Notebook* about heterosexual relationships, for example, or about politics or psychoanalysis.

Between 1958, when *A Ripple from the Storm* was published, and

1962, the year of *The Golden Notebook*, Lessing published an autobiographical narrative, *In Pursuit of the English* (1960), a volume of poetry, two plays – and short stories. Only one of her previous novels, *Retreat to Innocence* (1956), had been set in England. Did her failure to realise English life make her more careful about her next English novel? *Retreat* is the only novel that embarrasses Lessing; she is vehement in refusing permission to reprint it. (Its English subject is surely as much at issue as its supposed socialist realist slant or its non-autobiographical material.) That novel, the autobiographical narrative, the two plays and the stories can be described as trying out English settings and characters.[4] From one point of view, *The Golden Notebook* is Lessing's first successful novel about her 'adopted' country; in that novel her fiction, so to speak, catches up with her life. One of the plays, *Play with a Tiger* (1962), is virtually transcribed into *The Golden Notebook*. *A Man and Two Women*, published the year after the novel, contains stories published during the years Lessing was probably thinking about or actually composing *The Goiden Notebook*.

Up until this time Lessing's novels were spaced two years apart. Two more longish (for Lessing) spaces between novels have occurred so far in Lessing's career – the four years between *Landlocked* (1965) and *The Four-Gated City* (1969) and the five years between *The Memoirs of a Survivor* (1974) and *Shikasta* (1979). These separations should be noted; they suggest changes in gear – especially in a writer so prolific. *The Golden Notebook* is studded with reflections about and examples of short fiction. It is critical of the genre. This critique and the overlapping subject matter of the novel and the stories are the subject of my paper.

The Golden Notebook could be called a 'composite novel'[5] as well as a loosely woven collection of short stories and novellas. There are five notebooks (Black, Red, Yellow, Blue, Golden), three novels (one is complete, *Free Women*; the second in progress/unfinished, *The Shadow of the Third*; the third summarised, Saul Green's Algerian novel), and many short stories (the case of Jack Briggs, the story of the female swan, the story of Comrade Ted, Blood on the Banana Leaves, the story of the two executed soldiers, the story of Comrade Harry). There are many ideas, notes or motifs for short stories; the 19 entries in the Yellow 4 notebook are the major examples. Furthermore, if the diary/journal entries which occasionally appear in the Black and the Red notebook and always in the Blue notebook are considered stories, the list gets much longer. The letters Ella receives as the lonely hearts editor of a magazine can be described as another form of short story. Finally, it is also possible to perceive Anna's many dreams as short stories. They are usually brief, discrete narratives if that is one definition of the short story form. Thus, *The Golden Notebook* is an explosion of short fictions. The term 'composite' for its structure is remarkably apt.

Do the 19 asterisked ideas for stories in the Yellow 4 notebook accidentally duplicate the number of stories in *A Man and Two Women*? The number 19 becomes more emphatic when it appears in the title of the last story, 'To Room Nineteen'. I have no secret key to the number 19, but I can not help noticing its recurrence. Perhaps the recurrence is accidental, or perhaps it is a way of saying there are interrelationships here; look for them. Many of the stories do seem to comment on one another. Eleven of them are about men and women in conflict/attraction situations, primarily in England. (Only four are set in Africa.) Five or more could be described as triadic – about a man and two women, like the title story, and therefore echoic harbinger/reminders of Anna's novel in progress, *The Shadow of the Third*. Women in conflict/attraction with men is the major subject matter of the stories as it is a major, not the major, subject strand of *The Golden Notebook*.

Manipulation enters the male hunt for the female or the female hunt for the male. Some of the stories use the hunt framework with devastating results. In the first story, 'One Off the Short List', the point of view is the male hunter's. The story of his deteriorated marriage will be echoed in the final story of the deteriorated marriage of Susan and Matthew Rawlings. Two competent intelligent professionals marry, plan their children, begin to tire of one another. The man in each marriage begins to have affairs. Graham Spence chooses carefully planned affairs as his way of coping with existential emptiness; Susan Rawlings ultimately chooses suicide. The first and last stories in the collection form a painful counterpoint of male/female responses to failed marital/existential situations.

The woman hunter is unsuccessful, but more empathetically drawn than the male hunter. Maureen Watson survives the false dreams her mother has forced on her and tries instead to jump class through job and marriage. She cannot finally go through with her plan to marry Stanley Hunt and feels deserted by Tony Head (are they headhunters?), the man who sees her game and criticises her for it. The names suggest the representational character of these figures. The husband's final other woman in 'To Room 19' is Phil Hunt; Susan Rawlings in that story invents a lover named Michael Plant. Susan's name is not Maureen, but it could have been. Instead her husband is a Matthew and the lover she plants is a Michael. There is a Maureen Jeffries in 'Between Men', and a man who laments, 'Maureen, Maureen, Maureen, my lost love', in 'The New Man', but marries someone else. Mary is the named potter figure in 'The Two Potters'. Matthew Rawlings has his first affair with Myra Jenkins. Lessing's many novels have an A/M/J pattern of repetition, one related to gender roles and the fear of repetition.[6] In the stories, the M/J repetitions suggest fatality only; we choose the same partners again and again, and/or, we are all interchangeable.

This is part of the message in the names of the incestuous brother and sister, Fred and Freda, in 'Each Other' who are not explicitly identified as twins, but who are described as so alike we must consider them twins. In this story the triad is two men and a woman, a very rare pattern in Lessing's work. 'Notes for a Case History' contains both triads. It begins with two contrapuntal girls/women and their relation to the world and to males, then concentrates on Maureen and her relation to two men. Lessing spoofs the Freudian view that girls fall in love first and forever with their fathers and their brothers in 'How I Finally Lost My Heart'.

Perhaps Lessing's particular 'family romance' is a partial key to her preferred use of the two women, one man constellation. That constellation may represent her primal family. Three is the symbolic number for the family; it adds the child to the procreative two. Like Martha Quest, Lessing is a first born child, the second woman in a one man family – until her brother was born. It would be hard to describe Jonathan Quest as a significant brother figure; his existence is a statement of displacement, of how the mother favoured the son over the daughter. The family configuration that Lessing first experienced, that primal triad, has a preferred, almost obsessive, place in her fiction. The autobiographical families of this period repeat part of the primal pattern: Martha Quest has one daughter, Anna Wulf has one daughter (a significant selection/exclusion from the two boys, one girl Lessing herself bore).

The strongest man and two women stories in the collection are

'A Man and Two Women', 'Notes for a Case History', and 'To Room Nineteen'. Two others can be described as triadic, although the 'shadow of the third' is either absent or barely present: 'One Off the Short List' and 'Between Men'. Two of the four stories about children could be called stories about a man and two women. In 'Homage to Isaac Babel', a mother figure mediates between a young girl and a young boy; in 'The New Man', the point of view character is a young girl in a relation with the man who cries out for Maureen. In the most unusual man and two women story (unusual because it concerns art, not sexual dialectic and connects dream and waking life), 'The Two Potters', the female narrator mediates between the potter in her dreams and her potter friend, Mary Tawnish. (This story and 'A Room' suggest later novels; 'A Room' reads like notes for *Memoirs of a Survivor* [1974].)

Lessing's protagonists are characteristically 'other woman' figures who feel the presence of 'the shadow of the third', the wife, described in *The Golden Notebook* as 'the woman altogether better than I was' (p. 637).[7] In that novel, Ella's 'shadow' is Paul's Muriel, as Molly's is Richard's Marion, as Anna's is Michael's wife and the wives of her other men – Nelson, Jack, Maitland, De Silva, Milt, and so on. All of Anna's lovers, except Saul, are married and living with their wives. (Compare Martha Quest whose first and only passional affair comes during her second marriage and is with a married man.)

In 'A Man and Two Women', a wife figure actually invites her husband and her friend to become lovers; she even uses the phrase, *ménage à trois*. This unconventional triad becomes an actuality in *The Four-Gated City* (1969). Martha Quest, Lynda Coldridge and Mark Coldridge are the perfect *ménage à trois*. Martha, the other woman, feels no guilt, given the wife's asexuality and her acceptance of the sexually active Martha. This pattern is provocatively duplicated in *The Marriages Between Zones Three, Four, and Five* (1980) where once again the wife, Al·Ith, withdraws from the world in pursuit of esoteric knowledge and gives her functional place to Dabeeb. (Vahshi's role as Ben Ata's second wife and Arusi's stepmother is more formal than real.) These duplications/revisions of the primal triad in Lessing's fiction bear more extended analysis than I can give them here.

At least two stories have a 'shadow' fourth, the absent husband in 'A Man and Two Women', and the absent girlfriend in 'Each Other'. They function much like the thirds figures in standing for traditional or 'normal' coupling. The absent Philip belongs with Stella; his existence is a rein on Stella (compare the name with Ella/Anna) and Jack against Dorothy's desire (compare Dorothy Mellings in *The Good Terrorist*, [1985]) to cede Jack to Stella sexually so she can give herself completely to her newborn. Fred's absent girlfriend Alice is part of the cover the incestuous siblings present to the world.

Neither shadow thirds nor shadow fourths are foreground figures in their stories. They exist behind irregular relationships that are not supposed to be happening. These shadow figures can be correlated with Jungian notions of the shadow anima/animus, but I wish to assert another way of perceiving them. The wife figures who should be the 'real' partners are in fact 'shadow' partners. Thus, supposed social realities are in fact only apparent. Logically, therefore, the other woman should feel no guilt. In fact, of course, her guilt is there, an active part of her empathic response to the wife she wants to displace and usually has never even met.

One internal resemblance in *A Man and Two Women* is startling – the work the women do. They work in stage design, fabric design, commercial art, advertising. The media arts dominate this volume; Graham works on radio and TV, for example. There are no fiction writers, struggling, blocked or otherwise. The artists outside the media are few and emphatically not prose writers. Mary is a potter; Judith ('Our Friend Judith') and Johannes Potgieter ('A Letter Home') are poets. Against this background, the non-working Freda, fixed in her bedroom, and the once professional Susan Rawlings (who had worked in advertising) and is now a long-term housewife, stand out. The emphasis on the media arts in this volume is unique.

In *The Golden Notebook* Lessing deliberately creates a different dialectic betwen the blocked 'serious' writer and the media workers in TV, radio, film, newspaper, book and magazine publishing. In this novel she creates an ironic foreground dialectic out of what was implicit in *A Man and Two Women* – and confronts, for the first time in her career, a woman novelist. The over-prolific Lessing chooses for her central protagonist a novelist figure who can not write her next novel (so we are told, although she is writing *The Shadow of the Third* and all the notebooks) and downgrades the short stories she can write.

In the novel the protagonist's critical intelligence saves her sanity; in the stories 'intelligence' is sceptically evaluated. Its construction of an ideology of courtship, marriage and the family is bitterly mocked. Graham Spence's marriage, the Susan/Matthew marriage, the Maureen/Peggy/Tom courtship/marriage/adultery, the adultery/incest of Fred/Freda, the courtship strategies of Maureen/Shirley/Stanley, the adultery games of Graham, Matthew, Tom, Dorothy's invitation to adultery – all undercut both prevailing ideals of courtship, marriage and the family and 'progressive', 'intelligent' reconstructions of these ideals.

There is a significant exception. The woman Graham Spence decides to put on his short list, Barbara Coles, ultimately incurs his rage for having cased him perfectly. Her intelligence, like Maureen Watson's, is displayed in her insights into 'man and woman maneuvering – the great comic situation'.[8] The woman as well as the man are surely both victims in this not always so comic situation. The reader must be more sceptical about the powers of Barbara Coles, powers which permit her acquiesence in rape and other acts which satisfy Graham's needs. The woman seems the commodity in this story as she is in so many other stories in the collection, perhaps most obviously and most one-dimensionally in 'Woman on the Roof', where three workmen ritualistically watch a woman sun-bathing on a roof.

The short stories are not constructed to comment on themselves as fictional forms. *The Golden Notebook*, of course, could not have become a novel unless its compositor had decided to engage in what David Lodge calls a 'sceptical internal scrutiny' of 'the conventions of fictional realism'.[9] That scrutiny is accomplished in two major ways, by direct comment and by the juxtaposition of blocks of mixed narrative forms which overlap or conflict.

The word pastiche becomes a crucial term. James Shafter first uses a form of it in the Black 3 Notebook. '"Well, Anna, and how do you describe all this pastiching about?"' this fellow 'shafter' of the publishing world, asks her (p. 437). He is referring to the parody diary he and Anna have written together and successfully placed with a pretentious little magazine. (Compare their collaboration with the later collaboration of Anna and Saul.) He seems to be using pastiche in its older sense, one rarely used today, of satirical imitation of another artist or work. Anna uses it differently in the Yellow 4 Notebook.[10] When she completes her 19 asterisked ideas for short stories and novels, she writes, 'If I've gone back to pastiche, then it's time to stop' (p. 541). With these words, she closes the Yellow Notebook. Since this final instalment of the

Yellow Notebook is entirely taken up with the 19 story ideas, pastiche must refer to them in its second and more recent meaning of hodgepodge. The 19th entry, 'The Romantic Tough School of Writing', parodies American machismo writing and does suit the first/older meaning of pastiche. Anna's words, however, refer to all the entries and function to justify the closing of the notebook.

In fact, the fourth instalments of the Black, Red, and Yellow notebooks are formally congruent. Their brevity and their content are equated with sterility (p. 525). The Blue 4 notebook is not formally the same as the other notebooks, but all four of the fourth instalments of the notebooks are more conspicuously interrelated than they were before – a harbinger of their obliteration/unification in the Golden notebook. They are even more related two by two, the Black with the Red, the Yellow with the Blue.[11] The notebooks have also caught up with each other in time and with the present time of *Free Women*, 1957. In the Black 4 notebook, Anna dreams of a television version of the Mashopi group which she watches as an outsider; she is neither the script writer nor the director. The Red 4 notebook, like the Black 4, is filled with pasted in newspaper clippings and contains only one entry in Anna's handwriting. That entry is once again not Anna's story; it is Jimmy Shafter's story about Comrade Harry Mathews, the comrade who spends his life preparing for an interview with the global leader of communism, then Khrushchev, which will never happen and never could change the course of history (pp. 526–31).

Nineteen numbers are interpolated into the text of the Blue 4 notebook; the numbers are asterisked and enclosed in parentheses for the reader who wishes to look back to the Yellow 4 notebook to see if or how they correlate with the 19 story ideas headed by numbers and asterisks (but without parentheses). They more than correlate; they are interwoven into the narrative fabric of the story of Anna and Saul. What were 19 possibilities multiplied by the additional possibilities within each story (for instance, the characters could be English or American, writers or painters, suburban or bohemian, and so on) are reduced to/contained in the single story of Anna and Saul. All 19 story/novel ideas belong to Anna and Saul even when the interpolated numbers do not seem precisely placed in the woven narrative. The 19 Yellow notebook stories can be described as stories with a stable inner kernel of meaning and a provisional outer kernel. They sound remarkably like many of the stories in *A Man and Two Women*.

The first one opens: 'a woman, starved for love, meets a man rather younger than herself' (p. 531). The line could describe many women, but it also describes Anna. When the reader discovers in the Blue 4 notebook that Anna does meet a man younger than she who is named Saul, the story idea becomes either predictive or an example of the privileged omniscient knowledge the composite overall author alone has. The second story could have become 'One Off the Short List': 'A man uses grown-up language, the language of emotionally grown people, to gain a woman' (p. 531), but it becomes Saul's story. The third story, about a woman who falls in love with a man not worthy of her, is first imagined set in Africa, then 'this story translated into English terms' acquires a different outer kernel, but remains essentially the same story. The story seems removed from Anna's affair with Saul until we notice that Anna evaluates the so-called 'normal, the good men' as 'finished and completed and without potentialities' (p. 532). In this sense, then, story number 3 does describe Saul and explains Anna's preference for him over what others would call 'the normal, the good men'.

One could go on through all the 19 stories and see their correspondence with the Anna/Saul relationship. Number 13, about a 50-year-old man, is the most remote; it is not about Saul's present self, but it imagines one of his possible futures. Once a story character is named Annie (no. 3), another time Anna (no. 7); Mother Sugar appears in her own name (no. 11); another time, Anna's current lover merges for a moment with her former lover, Michael, of the *Free Women* and Blue Notebook sections (no. 10). Several times the male lover is identified as American, possibly American, or as an American ex-red (nos. 6, 9, 13, 15 and 19); either or both partners are described as sexually experienced or as rakes or he as a womaniser (nos. 3, 13, 16 and 17). Both keep diaries (nos. 7 and 14) which are finally as false as the ones Anna and Jimmy Shafter concocted – and meant to be, for the two are writing 'real' diaries which they hide from one another. The intensity of the man/woman interchange and separation duplicates the Anna/Saul pattern (nos. 4 and 18). The man's effect can be totally destructive; in one story (no. 8) the man feeds off the 'woman artist – painter, writer, doesn't matter which' (p. 534) – and leaves her when the artist in her is dead. Saul could have done this to Anna; instead he helps her to write again as she helps him to write. Saul could have committed suicide, like the American ex-red in story no. 9, as Anna could have – 'Anna committed suicide', the compositor imagines Saul writing in his false diary (no. 7). (Tommy's suicide attempt in *Free Women* fails; the young man's attempt in Ella's novel succeeds.) Instead of committing suicide, Saul and Anna go temporarily mad in the Blue 4 and the Golden notebooks and come out alive and changed.

These story ideas could have been turned into 19 separate stories; instead they were turned into the story of Anna and Saul. Lessing permits the reader access into the processes of story-making – how they gestate, how one idea is chosen over another, and so on. In their fixation on the sexual dialectic, the story ideas in the Yellow notebook are redolent of most of the 19 separate stories in *A Man and Two Women*. The Yellow notebook stories differ in one very important respect – they are about one woman and one man. Only one (no. 12) emphasises the two women, one man triad inscribed in the title of the short story collection.

The breaking of the primal triad in the Anna/Saul relationship seems to signal a victory over repetition, a victory over fatality. But is it? Milt, Saul's counterpart in the *Free Women* 5 section of *The Golden Notebook*, has the usual wife in the wings that all of Anna's other lovers have had. The differences between the Saul figure in Blue 4 and the Milt figure in *Free Women* 5 are part of a larger network of intertextual similarities and differences between these sections. The resultant oscillation provides the reader with deliberately constructed alternate endings to the complete novel, *The Golden Notebook*

Saul has no wife, but he has real and fictive other women whom he uses to excite Anna's jealousy and keep himself uncommitted. He has a relation with a Jane Bond when he first comes to live in Anna's house. He concocts women named Mavis, Marguerite, Dorothy in the diary entries he knows Anna will read (compare nos. 7 and 14). In the Blue 4 notebook, therefore, as in the other parts of the novel, the other woman continues to have the existence she lacks in the Yellow 4 notebook – although it is non-wifely and entirely fictive. Saul's other woman pointedly functions as his weapon against Anna; Saul creates her; she is not already there as wife figures always are. Anna's release from the primal triad inscribed in her relationship with Saul is, finally, only partial and temporary. 'Progress' is never whole or permanent in Lessing's work; it is emphatically provisional in *The Golden Notebook*.

The placement of the numbers and asterisks in parentheses in the Blue notebook sometimes seems out of place. An example: like the woman artist in story idea no. 8, Anna's 'whole life is oriented around an absent man for whom she is waiting' (p. 534). But the point in the Blue notebook where no. 8 appears does not seem quite the right place for it to appear, unless we interpret that waiting woman as 'the sick person who inhabited my body (no. 8) a while' (p. 561). However we construe the exactness of the correspondences between the 19 numbered items in the two places, Yellow and Blue, it would be hard not to agree that the 19 stories are indeed sewn into the Anna/Saul relationship.

The Blue notebook, which is supposed to be the notebook of truth, the notebook about Anna's 'real' life, becomes a rather shaky representative of truth and reality. If Yellow 4 presents story ideas which the compositor will weave together in the next notebook, the Blue 4, then how do we evaluate the material in Blue 4? If Blue 4 is based on story ideas, then how can it be the notebook of Anna's 'real' life?[12] Perhaps it too is fiction? Its credibility as reality seems seriously undermined.

Unlike Black, Red and Yellow 4, Blue 4 closes on a high note. It closes because something is about to be over and something new about to begin. Anna has left her flat and returned with a golden notebook. She resists her temptation to give it to Saul who asks for it: 'But I will not, I will not. I will not. I'll pack away the blue notebook with the others. I'll pack away the four notebooks. I'll start a new notebook, all of myself in one book' (p. 607). Blue 4 does not close because of sterility; it does not close because someone else is writing Anna's stories. While not yet her own producer, director or story teller, Anna is the weaver of the discrete story ideas of Yellow 4 into a whole. The fabric of Blue 4 contains events and meanings larger and more various than anything imagined in the negative sexual dialectics of the 19 earlier story ideas. Its depiction of Anna's merging selves, her recurrent dreams, her descent into volatile/cruel sexual behaviour ('sado-masochistic', p. 606) and madness with Saul not only unifies, but extends and explodes the material of Yellow 4. Saul's typically aggressive expropriation of the new notebook – he is the first to write in it and he calls it his book – becomes in fact a harbinger of the collaborative writing which will make both Anna and Saul writers again.

I propose the word montage for what Anna does in the Blue 4 notebook and again in the inner Golden notebook. Anna never uses the word, but it seems the apt counter to pastiche. First, it has a positive connotation that the word pastiche lacks. Second, it belongs to the film/TV lingo which is the metaphoric backbone of the inner Golden notebook. In that notebook, film techniques are reimagined positively, as distinct from the satiric evaluation of the film industry so much a part of the Black notebooks. Montage can, in fact, be described as a synonym for dream; all the montage scenes occur in Anna's dreams. Like dreams, montage can move freely in time and space. It can be described as dreaming awake. It can make wholes out of the hodgepodge associated with pastiche. It seems a metaphor for the power of the imagination.

Saul's injunction to Anna in the Blue 4 notebook, '"Instead of making a record of my sins in your diary, why don't you write another novel?"' (p. 604) is intensified in the Golden notebook. 'The disinterested personality who had saved me from disintegration', 'this controlling person' (at first a 'part of my mind', then a 'he') tells Anna 'that instead of making up stories about life, so as not to look at it straight, I should go back and look at scenes from my life' (p. 616). The larger inquiry into the relationship between life and fiction that is a constant in *The Golden Notebook* is at issue here. So is Anna's particular problem. The old innocent belief that only 'the good man', 'the whole man' can write the good/great work seems upheld here: Anna cannot write until she straightens herself out. The reverse is also paradoxically true as Saul insists; if Anna does not write, she will crack up or commit suicide. Writing is tied to her personal cure.

In *The Golden Notebook* stories qua stories acquire a psychological/moral dimension. They become a metaphor for 'fragmentation' and novels become a metaphor for 'unity'. (Lessing uses these words in her introduction to describe the poles of the novel.) This judgement is Anna Wulf's, the grand compositor of *The Golden Notebook,* not necessarily Doris Lessing's – although we know Doris Lessing sits somewhere behind Anna Wulf, paring her fingernails. Pastiche/story, finally, is to fragmention/division as montage/novel is to wholeness/unity. This equation implicates Anna in the usual 'higher' evaluation of the novel over the short story.

There is a possible irony. The conventional framing novel called *Free Women* is the only straightforward narrative in the composite novel. It has no interpolated short fictions, no letters, no diary entries, no flashbacks, no dreams. It never reflects on the limits of its form; it never breaks frame. Yet only the combination of its simple narrative with all the other unorthodox (incomplete, unpublished, and so on) short fictions approaches the complexity and contradiction of 'life', 'truth', or 'reality'. If we can imagine *Free Women* read consecutively through, it seems a laundered, tamer version of the materials in its companion interleaved notebooks. The reader is made privy to what it omits. Despite its unique apparently seamless character, therefore, it is not any closer to 'truth' than its companion sections.

The whole work largely sustains and only moderately undercuts Anna's judgement that the short story represents evasion or fragmentation and the 'seamless' novel its opposite. The composite novel defines truth as multiple, partial, problematic, shifting. The work of art cannot present experience in the way that women know it. Anna describes the simultaneity, the seamlessness of women's experience to Tommy in *Free Women* 2: 'That's how women see things. Everything is a sort of continuous creative stream' (p. 269). That mode of experience can be described as montage perfected. It can never be captured adequately in words. It can never exist fully in life. It is an ideal that art and life can only occasionally realise.

Only two of the stories in *A Man and Two Women* can be considered significant departures from the *Free Women* kind of narrative. These two stories, 'A Room' and 'The Two Potters', comment on art indirectly; they approach the fabular forms of Lessing's later fiction. The others pointedly share with *The Golden Notebook* the theme of destructive sexual dialectics. After these two works, Lessing's concentration on sexual dialectics abates and almost entirely disappears save for its elegiac reappearance in the fable form of *The Marriages Between Zones Three, Four, and Five* (1980) nearly 20 years later.

The incipiently composite character of *A Man and Two Women* becomes the self-conscious organising principle of *The Golden Notebook*. Narrative forms proliferate – short story, parody, film script, diary, letter, headline, synopsis, news clipping – and tend to comment on themselves. Instead of duplicate Maureens, there is a central protagonist, Anna, and her other selves, female (Molly, Marion, Maryrose, Ella, Mrs Marks), and male (two Pauls, Michael, Max, Milt, Tommy, Saul). One could be extravagant and say the 19 stories of *A Man and Two Women* are to *The Golden Notebook* as the 19 ideas of the Yellow 4 notebook are to their interweaving in the Blue notebook – except that the principle of organisation in *The Golden Notebook* is not interweaving but parallel or side by side discourse which approaches unity in the fourth notebook instalments and in the Golden notebook. *The Golden Notebook* can be described as pastiche turned to deliberate advantage. Then the novel is both pastiche and montage?

The title/story of *A Man and Two Women* also ties the two works together in pointing to a specifically recurring feature of the woman/man interaction in both. Lessing's recurring triadic relationships in her stories and her novels have an obsessive quality. Other themes acquire a stronger light when these two works are considered together. The elaborate distancing/displacement of the suicide theme in *The Golden Notebook* into other characters – 'real' and fictive – is an example. Does 'the happy philosophy', as socialism is ironically called in the Black 3 notebook, make it too hard for Anna to confront her own suicidal impulses? (p. 428).

Looking at the short stories in *The Golden Notebook* forces us to re-examine the interaction of the Yellow 4 and the Blue 4 notebooks, for the 19 story ideas in Yellow 4 that are sewn into Blue 4 invite comparative comment about these two notebooks, their relation to the remaining fourth instalments and their relation to the 19 stories of *A Man and Two Women*. This analysis of the fourth notebook entries clarifies their pattern and meaning, their readiness for obliteration/unification in the Golden notebook which follows.

The expansion/weaving of the 19 stories into the single narrative of Blue 4 seems an open invitation to us to see how story ideas can become part of a single structure. The secondary invitation is highly provocative. We seem forced to evaluate the short story ideologically, as one of the many forms of fragmentation described in the novel. The reverse is also potentially true, since the pattern of the overall *Golden Notebook* is composite rather than woven. Perhaps the novel learned how to adapt the inconclusiveness of the 'free story' ending to itself?[13] In providing her readers with the different shapes of the 19 story ideas in the Yellow 4 and Blue 4 notebooks or the alternate endings of the Blue 4 and *Free Women* 5 sections, Lessing insists on the 'indeterminacy' (Hanson p. 14) which characterises her short stories.

Notes

1. My thanks to Ann Lane and Ron Lopez for help in arriving at a title.
2. Hugh Walker, *The Literature of the Victorian Era* (Cambridge, 1913) p. 745. Quoted by Gordon Haight, Introduction to *Middlemarch*, (Boston: Houghton, Mifflin, 1956) xv.
3. Linda Weinhouse is the only critic I know to have speculated on the relationship between *A Man and Two Women* and *The Golden Notebook*. She argues that 'Each Other' is the only story in *A Man and Two Women* 'crucial to an understanding of *The Golden Notebook*'. 'Crucial' is exaggerated, but Weinhouse's insight into the connection between the two works is valuable. See '"Each Other" and *The Golden Notebook*' in 'Doris Lessing and Incest' (Ph.d. dissertation, Hebrew University, Jerusalem, 1983).

   The only sustained examination of *A Man and Two Women* is Margaret Atack's superb analysis of the oppositional structures in the stories – their encounters between the self and others, between men and women, between desire and refusal, and so on. See 'Towards A Narrative Analysis of *A Man and Two Women*' in *Notebooks/Memoirs/Archives: Reading and Rereading Doris Lessing*, ed. Jenny Taylor (London: Routledge & Kegan Paul, 1982) pp. 135–63.
4. See Molly Hite, who calls these works 'rehearsals' for *The Golden Notebook*, in 'In Pursuit of the Author: Doris Lessing's Rehearsals for *The Golden Notebook*,' an unpublished paper presented at the 1986 Modern Language Association Convention.
5. Elizabeth Abel, '*The Golden Notebook*: "Female Writing" and "The Great Tradition,"' in Claire Sprague and Virginia Tiger (eds), *Critical Essays on Doris Lessing* (Boston: G. K. Hall, 1986) pp. 101–107.
6. For further discussion of Lessing's recurrent A/M/J naming patterns, see Claire Sprague, *Rereading Doris Lessing: Narrative Strategies of Doubling and Repetition* (Chapel Hill: University of North Carolina Press, 1987).
7. *The Golden Notebook* (New York: Bantam, [1962] 1973).
8. *A Man and Two Women* (New York: Simon & Schuster, [1963] 1984) p. 27.
9. 'Keeping Up Appearances', [Review of *Summer Before The Dark*] *New Statesman*, 14 May 1973. Reprinted in *Doris Lessing*, ed. Eve Bertelsen (Johannesburg: McGraw-Hill, 1985) p. 81.
10. Lessing does not number the notebook instalments as she does the *Free Women* instalments: 1, 2, 3, 4, 5. I find the addition of numbers to each notebook instalment too useful to resist.
11. This pattern of two by two superseded by a fifth is, of course, noticeable in the first four volumes of the Martha Quest quintet whose first two depict Martha immersed in the family she was born into and the one she makes by marriage and whose last two depict her immersion in the political group/family she joins. The final fifth novel breaks the patterns of the earlier four as the golden fifth breaks the limits of the four notebooks.
12. While reading Saul's diary in Blue 4, Anna comes across an entry 'she

had already written. . . , in my yellow notebook' which she attributes to 'some awful second sight'. That is her way of seeing it. We can also ask, if fictional yellow predicts true blue, then is blue true? *The Golden Notebook*, p. 572.

13. Hanson, Clare, 'Free Stories: The Shorter Fiction of Doris Lessing', *Doris Lessing Newsletter* 9, 1 (1985) p. 7.

11

Crystals, Fragments and Golden Wholes: Short Stories in *The Golden Notebook*

ELLEN CRONAN ROSE

Doris Lessing is a self-confessed short story junkie. 'Some writers I know', she says in the Preface to *African Stories*, "have stopped writing short stories because . . . "there is no market for them." Others like myself, the addicts, go on, and I suspect would go on even if there really wasn't any home for them but a private drawer.'[1]

I hope here to define the achievement of *The Golden Notebook* by approaching it via the volume of short stories Lessing published a year later, *A Man and Two Women*.[2] The relationship between these two books, I will argue, both highlights the central concerns of the novel and prevents critical closure of it. Moreover, the intertextuality of the short stories and the novel provides a model by which to understand Lessing's unique contribution to contemporary literature and appreciate her special genius. Serendipitously, this study of *The Golden Notebook* may also suggest why Lessing is addicted to writing short stories.

Lessing has said that the difference between short stories and novels is that 'a novel tends to be a long process and a short story something small crystallising out'.[3] Elizabeth Abel brilliantly uses one of the stories in *A Man and Two Women* to clarify a pivotal thematic and structural feature of *The Golden Notebook*. In 'Each Other', she argues, something in Lessing's long process of contemplating the embattled relations between the sexes crystallises into a vision of an egalitarian (hetero)sexuality that defiantly challenges patriarchy's 'central social law' of exogamy. The brother-sister incest of 'Each Other' resonates within *The Golden Notebook* both in the Black Notebook's subplot of Maryrose's passionate love for her brother and in the inner Golden Notebook, when Anna thinks of Saul 'as if he were my brother'. This, 'the sexual telos toward which the novel works', both rescues Anna from 'her futile round of self-destructive relationships' and 'empowers' her as a writer.[4]

Illuminating as this reading is, it must not tempt us to reduce *The Golden Notebook* to the crystalline lisibility of 'Each Other'. Nor will we be so tempted if we follow Abel's example and read the other stories in *A Man and Two Women* in the context of *The Golden Notebook*; we will discover that almost half of the stories echo or are echoed in the novel.

The triangle of the implicit, potential *ménage à trois* of the title story can be imposed on group after group of characters in *The Golden Notebook*. As in 'A Man and Two Women', the junctures of this triangle are variously charged: the women may compete for the man or ally themselves against him; 'the shadow of the third' may threaten or enable the extramarital affair; the presence of a man may disrupt conversation between women or instigate it. Elements of another story, 'Dialogue', appear in Blue Notebook 4 and the inner Golden Notebook, underscoring Anna's ambivalent relationship to Saul Green.

Despite the strong colouring cast by these and the initial story, 'One Off the Short List', the stories in *A Man and Two Women* do not deal exclusively with the war between the sexes, nor are they all set in England. Yet when one of the 'African' stories in the collection makes its way into *The Golden Notebook*, it does not end up where one might expect to find it, in the Black Notebook. The dung beetles of 'The Sun Between Their Feet', no less than Sisyphus, are avatars of Paul Tanner / Michael / Anna's boulder pushers.

In *Free Women* 4, Anna tells Marion an African story in an attempt to make her see how unrealistic her 'pretence of caring about African nationalism' is, how much a fantasy constructed to help her avoid confronting the harsh reality that her marriage to Richard has been a hollow sham.[5] Anna's story is a version of Lessing's 'Outside the Ministry', where the 'saintly', 'hardworking' Mr Kwenzi is contrasted with the dissipated, incompetent Mr Devuli, who will nonetheless 'certainly be elected' Minister when their state is granted independence by Britain ('Outside the Ministry', pp. 230–2).

This inventory of correspondences between *A Man and Two Women* and *The Golden Notebook* comprises a virtual catalogue of the themes readers since 1962 have detected in and celebrated the novel for: the troubled relationship between the sexes, the postulated centrality of a woman's point of view, the fragility of sanity, the soured idealism of left-politics. But while these are themes Lessing has acknowledged her interest in they are not, she is right to insist, central to *The Golden Notebook*. That is because the central theme of *The Golden Notebook* is neither political nor psychological, but epistemological. It is, to borrow Lessing's words, about discovering the 'unity' beneath and within the 'fragmentation' of experiential reality (GN p. xi). Because this theme challenges the reality of experience and thus calls representation itself into question, it can be expressed only through form and Lessing hoped, in *The Golden Notebook*, 'to shape a book which would make its own comment, a wordless statement: to talk through the way it was shaped' (GN p. xvii).

The formal relationship between *A Man and Two Women* and *The Golden Notebook* is similar to and draws our attention to relationships between elements of the novel – between a variety of 'stories' or 'story ideas' and the larger fictions in which they are embedded. For that reason, and not because their content resembles the content of *The Golden Notebook*, certain of these stories can help us hear the wordless articulation of *The Golden Notebook's* central theme.

The most obvious difference between a story in *A Man and Two Women* and its reinscription in *The Golden Notebook* is that in the collection it retains its integrity, while in the novel it is encroached on and utilised by the surrounding text. There is a sequence in Yellow Notebook 3, for example, which parallels one of Lessing's favourite stories from *A Man and Two Women*, 'One Off the Short List'. After Paul leaves Ella, her boss Dr West proposes an affair and, when she refuses, 'remarks spitefully: "There are others, you know. You aren't condemning me to solitude." ' Ella 'understands' that 'he will work through a short list of three or four women' (GN p. 386).

If a phrase from this episode reminds us of the story's title, details from the anecdote Julia tells (GN pp. 386–7) to 'cap' Ella's about Dr West tie this section of the Yellow Notebook even more firmly to 'One Off the Short List'. Julia is an actress; her story therefore comes from the same milieu as Barbara Coles's. Like

Coles, Julia offers a man who has brought her home a cup of coffee and discovers that he won't leave until he has bedded her. Like Coles, Julia gives in out of pure exhaustion; like Graham Spence, the man is impotent.

At the same time, as Ella and Julia continue to trade stories about the sexual battle zone mapped so clearly by the story, this episode reminds us of another story of jaded sexuality, 'Between Men'. Like Maureen Jeffries and Peggy Bayley, Ella and Julia resume a friendship on the basis of their mutual 'criticism of men' and wonder whether this means they are 'Lesbian, psychologically if not physically' (GN p. 389).

In *A Man and Two Women*, 'One Off the Short List' and 'Between Men' are physically separated by eight stories; a reader may *choose* to see them in relation to each other but is not encouraged to do so by the disposition of stories within the volume. Each can be analyzed in terms of its self-defined perimeter of signification.[6]

But when 'One Off the Short List' is written into *The Golden Notebook*, it is intertwined with 'Between Men'. This effectively alters both stories: it provides the pretext for Maureen Jeffries's and Peggy Bayley's disenchantment with men and provides Barbara Coles with a confidante to whom she can relate her outrageous evening with Graham Spence. Moreover, both stories are absorbed into the story of Ella's relationship with Julia and their unsatisfying experiences with men.

The intertextuality of 'One Off the Short List', 'Between Men' and *The Golden Notebook* is further complicated by the fact that Ella and Julia are characters in a story written by Anna Wulf, while Barbara Coles, Maureen Jeffries and Peggy Bayley figure in stories written by Doris Lessing.

Of course, although within *The Golden Notebook* Anna Wulf is represented as the author not only of the novel-in-progress about Ella called *The Shadow of the Third*, but also of the five notebooks, *Frontiers of War, Free Women* and – arguably – *The Golden Notebook*, ultimately Doris Lessing is the source of all these fictions.[7] This has disconcerting effects on the representational verisimilitude of *The Golden Notebook*, effects the text exploits in order to question traditional distinctions between life and art.

In *The Golden Notebook* the relationship between 'fiction' and 'reality' is figured, in part, by the relationship between Anna Wulf and her character Ella, who is also a writer. During the course of the Yellow Notebook, Ella completes a novel about a suicidal young man, then 'looks inside herself' for other stories to write. She 'finds' one about a woman 'over-ready for a serious love' who falls in love with a man who 'is playing at the role of a serious lover because of some need for asylum or refuge'. As their affair proceeds, the woman becomes unreasonably and unprecedentedly jealous. 'Ella looked at this story with amazement; because there was nothing in her own experience that could suggest it. . . . Perhaps I read it somewhere? – she wonders' (GN pp. 394–5).

According to the conventions of realist fiction, Ella could not have read that story, because it is written – or plotted – by her creator, Anna Wulf, in Yellow Notebook 4, a collection of plot outlines and story ideas, as '*6 A Short Story' about 'A man and a woman, in a love affair. She, for hunger of love, he for refuge' (GN p. 456) which, we learn in Blue Notebook 4, comes not out of Ella's story but from Anna's experience with Saul Green. If it is disconcerting to think of the character Ella's imagined stories being shaped by her creator Anna's experience, which is presumably external to the textual universe Ella inhabits, it is positively disorienting to realise that Anna's experience is prefigured by a story her character imagines. 'Looking for outlines of a story and finding, again and again, nothing but patterns of defeat, death, irony', Ella decides she must 'accept the patterns of self-knowledge which mean unhappiness or at least a dryness. But I can twist it into victory. A man and a woman – yes. Both at the end of their tether. Both cracking up because of a deliberate attempt to transcend their own limits. And out of the chaos, a new kind of strength' (GN pp. 399–400). Within the fiction she inhabits, Ella neither writes this story nor has the kind of experience it describes. Its images take on form and life only in Blue Notebook 4 and the inner Golden Notebook, to record the experience of Anna Wulf and Saul Green.

If Ella can not write that story, there are others she refuses to write because 'she is afraid that writing [them] might make [them] come true' (GN p. 394). Part of Yellow Notebook 3 suggests that there is a direct connection, if not a strictly causal relationship, between stories and life. Frustrated by her father's refusal to give her details of his marriage to her mother, Ella is forced as it were to imagine them. In the 'story' that 'shapes itself' in her imagination, her father takes on the character 'of a man who might have been a poet or mystic. And in fact, when he died, journals, poems, fragments of prose are found in locked drawers'. Ella is 'surprised by this conclusion' because 'she had never thought of her father as a man who might write poetry, or write at all'. Yet when she asks him if he has ever written poetry, he opens a locked drawer and hands her, as Ella's dream predicted, a 'sheaf of poems' (GN pp. 397–8). Though to be sure, Ella's story did not make a poet out of her father, it did give her an insight into his character which 35 years of being his daughter had not yielded.

The force of this anecdote is intensified when we recall Jimmy McGrath's father from Black Notebook 1, like Ella's father a 'retired Indian Colonel' who drinks more than is good for him and writes poems (GN p. 74). Ella's father seems to have been created by Anna Wulf to demonstrate the prophetic or heuristic value of story-telling: Ella has learned the 'truth' about the 'real' character (Colonel McGrath) on whom Anna Wulf modelled Ella's 'fictional' father. Or perhaps the point is being made by the author who created Colonel McGrath in the first place, Doris Lessing.

For it was Doris Lessing, not Anna Wulf, who included in *A Man and Two Women* the enigmatic story, 'Two Potters', in which the narrator's unfolding dream story of an African potter inter-penetrates the life of her friend Mary, a real potter. Mary, introduced as someone who does not dream, avidly follows the 'installments' of her friend's dream ('Two Potters' p. 148). When the narrator tells her the potter, 'tired with long centuries of making pots', has fashioned a clay rabbit he wants God to 'breathe life into', Mary protests: 'Why a rabbit? I simply don't *see* a rabbit' (p. 151). The narrator bristles. It's *her* story, not Mary's. But is it? The dream stops, and the narrator realises 'it was because of my effrontery in creating that rabbit, inserting myself into the story' (p. 152). So she turns her attention to Mary, whose life takes up elements of the dream story and gives them unexpected twists. Mary starts making clay rabbits 'for the children' (p. 152), which leads to a confrontation between rationalism (embodied by Mary's scientist husband) and imagination (represented by the children's 'play'). And Mary enters the play, not only by humouring her son but also by crafting a rabbit for the potter in the dream story, a clay 'animal far more in keeping with the dried mud houses, the dusty plain, than the pretty furry rabbit' her friend had incorrectly dreamed (p. 156). In a final mystification of the distinction between dream story and real life, the narrator gives the fictional African potter in her dream the real clay rabbit Mary has crafted and it 'jumps' off his palm 'with quick, jerky movements' (p. 159). In this story, which blurs the distinctions between fact and fiction, the dreamer / story teller discovers the mysterious subtext of her potter friend Mary, outwardly unimaginative and placid, inwardly rebellious, ludic, anarchic.[8]

The vertiginous interplay of fiction and fact, stories and life prefigured by 'Two Potters' is, in *The Golden Notebook*, nowhere more intense than in the two notebooks immediately preceding the inner Golden Notebook. Anna's novel about Ella effectively ends with Yellow Notebook 3. The fourth and final section of the Yellow Notebook comprises 19 plot outlines or story ideas, each identified by an asterisk and a number. In Blue Notebook 3, Anna describes the function of each of her four notebooks; she uses the Yellow Notebook to 'make stories' of her experience, while the Blue Notebook 'tries to be a diary' (GN p. 406). Thus it makes sense that the plot outlines and story ideas of Yellow Notebook 4 are intercalated by numbered asterisks with Blue Notebook 4. What does not make immediate sense is the connection between the stories Anna outlines in the Yellow Notebook and the experience she is living through in the Blue Notebook, although they are loosely analogous, having to do with the problematic, even neurotic, symbiosis between two political, sexual beings. But often there is no apparent relationship between the story Anna constructs in the Yellow Notebook and the experience she is (presumably concurrently) having with Saul.

Pages 479–80 of Blue Notebook 4, for example, record an idyllic period in Saul and Anna's relationship. This account is punctuated by four numbered asterisks, directing us to stories 5, 6, 7 and 8 in Yellow Notebook 4, all of them about failed communication and sexual betrayal. Directly after Anna writes, in the Blue Notebook, 'I can say nothing about it [the past week] except that I was happy', she adds '*6' in parentheses. Story *6 in the Yellow Notebook is about a man who lies to a woman about his affairs with other women.

Anna says in the Blue Notebook that she knows that Saul is deceiving her *because* she has written story *6:

> Last evening he said: "I have to go and see . . ." a long complicated story followed. . . . I knew what it was all about, of course, but I didn't want to know and that in spite of the fact that I had written the truth in the yellow diary. [GN p. 480. The first ellipsis is in the text; the second is mine]

But when did she 'know'? When did she write the story? The language of the Blue Notebook is confusing on this score: 'Then he said, sullen and hostile: "You are very permissive, aren't you?" He had said it yesterday, and I wrote in the yellow notebook' (GN p. 480). 'Yesterday', according to the time scheme established by the Blue Notebook, was after the week-long idyll. That suggests that Anna 'experienced' a week of uncomplicated love with Saul and recorded it in the Blue Notebook; that at its conclusion, on the basis of additional experience, she wrote some story outlines in the Yellow Notebook; that, bitter and disillusioned, she then went back to the Blue Notebook and 'annotated' it to reflect her subsequent knowledge about its aftermath.

Or did part of Anna know, while she was 'happy', that such happiness was illusory? Choosing not to 'hear' Saul in the Blue Notebook, did Anna use the Yellow Notebook to register what she in fact heard and could not totally pretend not to have heard? Anna says she has written 'the truth' in the Yellow Notebook. Is the Blue Notebook's presentation of that week, then, a fiction?

Where does Anna's knowledge come from, experience or imagination? With Anna, we wonder what kind of knowledge writing stories manifests. Is it, as Anna suggest, 'second sight' or 'intuition' (GN p. 489)? Did she learn something about Saul by writing a story imagined at a time when her experience with him contradicted everything the story says?

In Yellow Notebook 3, Ella and her father talk about the novel she has just written about the young man who commits suicide. 'Poor stick', her father says, 'What did he want to kill himself for?' Ella answers, 'Perhaps because something was owed to him'. Her father is outraged. 'Perhaps, you say? Perhaps? You wrote it, so you ought to know' (GN pp. 398–9). Most of us are like Ella's father. We believe that authors 'know' the outcomes of their stories before they write them. But Ella, as we have seen, learns things that surprise her through the stories she writes. Similarly, Anna Wulf does not 'understand what happens at the moment Ella separates herself from me and becomes Ella' (GN p. 393), a character in a story which, possibly, discovers things about Anna's relationship with Michael she did not know while she was living it.

The Golden Notebook is studded with examples of characters who learn through writing or write in order to learn. Sometimes Anna learns something by writing about it in one or another of her diaries. But more often the multiple authors of the novel learn through writing stories. When Paul the psychiatrist learns that Ella is writing a novel about a suicide, he offers her details from his clinical practice; she prefers 'to write the book, to see what will happen' (GN p. 180). Similarly, Anna rejects statements of fact about Willi in favour of describing him 'so that a reader can feel [his] reality'. This teaches her both that fiction is 'amoral' and that she does not care, because 'the human personality, that unique flame', is 'sacred' to her (GN pp. 67–8). Near the end of the inner Golden Notebook Anna starts plotting a short story or novella, and stops in chagrin when she realises she is doing what she (and Ella) have often done, 'creating' "the third" – the woman altogether better than I was'. But this time she goes further than either she or Ella had been able to go before: she begins to think 'that quite possibly these marvellous, generous things we walk side by side with in our imaginations could come in existence, simply because we need them, because we imagine them' (GN p. 545). When she tells Saul this story he says, 'We've got to believe in our beautiful impossible blueprints' (GN p. 546). He also says she should start writing fiction again. Brushing aside her excuses, he forces her to take up a pencil and then dictates the first sentence of what he assures her will be her next book.

As we know, the sentence Saul dictates is the first sentence of *Free Women*, and most critics of *The Golden Notebook* agree that *Free Women* demonstrates that Anna Wulf has conquered her writers' block and, coincidentally, analysed and conquered at least some of the sexual, political and artistic demons whose torments the notebooks record. Most critics also quote Lessing to assert that 'this small neat thing', this 'conventional' short novel, is less 'true' than the 'rough and apparently formless and unshaped' experience – that is, the notebooks – from which it has been distilled (GN p. xvii).

When Lessing wrote the Introduction to *The Golden Notebook* in 1971, she was trying to correct nine years of misreading by reviewers and academic critics who claimed it was about 'the sex war' or 'politics' or 'mental illness'. 'Yet the essence of the book', she insisted, 'the organisation of it, everything in it, says implicitly and explicitly, that we must not divide things off, must not compartmentalize' (GN p. xiv). Critics are still compartmentalising *The Golden Notebook*, ironically *because* they listened to Lessing's injuction in the 1971 Introduction to pay attention to its form. They contrast *Free Women* to *The Golden Notebook* in order to dismiss the former; celebrating the innovative, kaleidoscopic structure of *The Golden Notebook*, they fail to reflect that a kaleidoscope creates its endless patterns by shifting small pieces of glass in relation to each other. *The Golden Notebook* is a novel constructed by the play of one story against another; all are necessary, none insignificant.

The authors in *The Golden Notebook* learn through writing; so did the author of it. 'All sorts of ideas and experiences I didn't recognise as mine emerged when writing', Lessing says. She then speculates that 'perhaps giving oneself a tight structure, making limitations for oneself, squeezes out new substance where you least expect it'. Finally, she describes writing *The Golden Notebook* as a 'crystallising process' (GN p. xiv). This language recalls Lessing's statement, cited earlier in this essay, that a short story is 'something small crystallising out'.

The Golden Notebook opens with the sentence Saul Green dictates to Anna Wulf. It, not *Free Women*, embodies the theme of fragmentation he also dictated ('There are the two women you are, Anna' [GN p. 547]). 'In the inner Golden Notebook', Lessing says, 'things have come together, the divisions have broken down, there is formlessness with the end of fragmentation – the triumph of the second themes, which is that of unity' (GN p. xi). Why, then, did Lessing not conclude her novel with the inner Golden Notebook? Why did she end, instead, with the concluding section of that small, neat conventional novel, *Free Women*? Why did she follow *The Golden Notebook* with a collection of short stories, *A Man and Two Women*, in which the inchoate mass of *The Golden Notebook* is further fragmented and crystallised, freezing the motion picture to which Anna likens the experience recorded in *The Golden Notebook* into a series of still shots? One might as well ask why Lessing followed her first, African novel with a collection of African stories; interrupted *Children of Violence*, which takes Martha Quest from Africa to London, with one volume of novellas and another of short stories divided between African and British settings; why she played with science fiction motifs in a volume of short stories and a short novel about a crystal from outer space before embarking on her current voyage to Canopus in Argos.

The Golden Notebook demonstrates formally what this survey of her corpus was meant to suggest – that Doris Lessing is a novelist for whom writing short stories is not a sideline but a necessary part of her total creative enterprise. Stories are ways of knowing, portals of discovery, opportunities to pause in the long process of a novel to crystallise a character, a mood, a theme.

Like Anna Wulf, Lessing left the Communist Party in the 1950s, disillusioned by Hungary and the 20th Congress. But she retained Marxism's dialectic as her characteristic, habitual epistemology. Either/or thinking is alien to her; as Charles Watkins says in *Briefing for a Descent into Hell*, 'it isn't either or at all, it's and, and, and, and, and, and' for Lessing.[9] *The Golden Notebook* is her quintessential crystallisation of both/and: stories and diaries and pastiches, Anna and Ella and the shadow of the third, the small neat *Free Women* and the chaos of the notebooks from which it emerges. And in *The Golden Notebook*, she reveals the complementarity of the novels and short stories that comprise her *oeuvre*. She calls it the naming game:

> First I created the room I sat in, object by object, "naming" everything, bed, chair, curtains, till it was whole in my mind, then move out of the room, creating the house, then out of the house, slowly creating the street, then rise into the air, looking down on London . . . then slowly, slowly, I would create the world, continent by continent . . . (but the point of "the game" was to create this vastness while holding the bedroom, the house, the street in their littleness in my mind at the same time) until the point was reached where I moved out into space. . . . Then, having reached that point, with the stars around me, and the little earth turning underneath me, I'd try to imagine at the same time, a drop of water, warming with life, or a green leaf. Sometimes I could reach what I wanted, a simultaneous knowledge of vastness and of smallness. [GN p. 469; ellipses mine]

The Golden Notebook is one of those magical moments.

Notes

1. Doris Lessing, 'Preface,' *African Stories* (New York: Ballantine, 1966), p. x.
2. Doris Lessing, *A Man and Two Women* (New York: Popular Library, 1963). References to stories from this edition will be incorporated parenthetically in the text.
3. Eve Bertelsen, 'Interview with Doris Lessing', in *Doris Lessing*, ed. Eve Bertelsen (Isando, SA: McGraw Hill, 1985) p. 103.

4. I am quoting in this paragraph from Elizabeth Abel, 'Resisting the Exchange: Brother-Sister Incest in Fiction by Doris Lessing', in *Doris Lessing: The Alchemy of Survival*, ed. Carey Kaplan and Ellen Cronan Rose (Athens: Ohio Univ. Press. 1988).
5. Doris Lessing, *The Golden Notebook* (New York: Simon and Schuster, 1962) p. 436. I am using the 1972 third printing, which includes Lessing's 1971 Introduction.
6. Margaret Atack, for example, brilliantly discloses the discursive practice of several of the stories. See her 'Towards a Narrative Analysis of *A Man and Two Women*', in *Notebooks / Memoirs / Archives: Reading and Rereading Doris Lessing*, ed. Jenny Taylor (Boston and London: Routledge & Kegan Paul, 1982) pp. 135–63.
7. The argument that Anna is author of *The Golden Notebook* is convincingly advanced by Joseph Hynes. See 'The Construction of *The Golden Notebook*', *The Iowa Review* vol. 4 (Summer 1973) no. 3, pp. 100–13.
8. Thanks to Carey Kaplan for insisting I take 'another look' at this story which, at first glance, I thought bore no relationship to *The Golden Notebook*.
9. Doris Lessing, *Briefing for a Descent into Hell* (New York: Knopf, 1971) p. 165.